With all best

In My End

Diana Baynes Jansen

www.newgeneration-publishing.com

New Generation Publishing

Old men ought to be explorers
Here or there does not matter
We must be still and still moving
Into another intensity
For a further union, a deeper communion
Through the dark cold and the empty desolation,
The wave cry, the wind cry, the vast waters
Of the petrel and the porpoise. In my end is my beginning

T.S.Eliot: *The four Quartets: East Coker. (Lines 382-389)*

My Beginning

Evie D'Oyly with Diana

Contents

Prologue 1

Part One 9

    Chapter 1: In the Beginning 9

    Chapter 2: Another Era 31

    Chapter 3: School 42

    Chapter 4: Cambridge 56

    Chapter 5: Holidays 67

    Chapter 6: Cranborne Chase 82

    Chapter 7: The New World 93

    Chapter 8: St Thomas' 104

Part Two 112

    Chapter 9: Marriage 112

    Chapter 10: Married Life and Singing 126

    Chapter 11: Family Life 140

    Chapter 12: America 152

    Chapter 13: Home Again 165

    Chapter 14: Another Chapter 177

    Chapter 15: Life Continues 191

Part Three 197

    Chapter 16: A Second Marriage 197

    Chapter 17: France 212

    Chapter 18: Parkinson's Disease 221

Chapter 19: Final Chapter 237

Chapter 20: Life After Death....................................... 244

Epilogue.. 246

Our Families 246

Introduction

The writing of this autobiography has been an exercise in getting to know myself, an attempt, perhaps, to reflect on my life from a more objective standpoint, as though I have been writing a biography. In this, I have been helped and inspired by the autobiography of Clare Tomalin, *A Life of My Own*, who is such an accomplished writer of other people's lives. In her writing, Clare is refreshingly honest and has not wanted to make out that her life has been any better or happier than in fact it was; it feels like an unvarnished account of the way things really were, both in her relationships and her life experiences, and this is what I too have attempted to portray.

Looking at my life now, with the hind sight of 82 years, I see it as a patchwork of light and dark, successes and failures, great happiness as well as profound sadness. I have tried not to gloss over the difficult bits and nor do I want to under estimate the deep love and happiness I have experienced. Both the grief and the happiness are a part of the whole picture. In writing of the events and relationships which have created the person that I am now, I have written about things I have not discussed with anyone and it is a little like opening one's most private inner world for everyone to see. It feels somewhat alarming, but on the other hand, it is now all in the past and I feel ready to share what has been, in the hope that it will help me to become something more than the result of the outer experiences of a life time, and that in this last chapter of life my end will truly be my beginning; the two will become one!

Acknowledgements

I have been helped by so many of my family and friends in the writing of this memoir. First, I would like to thank my mother, whose warm and guiding presence has been with me throughout the writing of the book and she has been a profound influence on my entire life, although, sadly, she is no longer here to read what I have written.

I give my thanks also to all those who have been an essential part of my life and who have helped me to become the person I am now:

To my husband, David, who gave me the happiest years of my life as well as my three wonderful daughters.

To my second husband, Chris, who brought so much joy and such rich experiences into my life, as well as the gift of his four splendid sons.

To my three daughters, Nicola, Helena and Catherine, by whose lives I am so enriched and to their children who bring me such great joy. All have had a profound influence on the writing of this book.

My special thanks to my daughter, Nicola, who did a very splendid first edit of the book together with much advice as to what to leave out!

My thanks also to my step son, Justin Jansen, for the many beautiful photographs of our family, taken by him, which are included in this memoir.

My thanks to Jane Torday, for reading the manuscript and for giving me warm encouragement.

A big thank you also to Joanna Eade, (friend of my nephew, Jonathan Baynes, the outstanding editor of my first book; *Jung's Apprentice*), for giving the book a professional final edit.

Prologue

> There was a considerable age difference between my parents. It was my father's fourth marriage; he was twenty-one years older than my mother. When they married my father was 49 and my mother was 28.
>
> Helton Godwin Baynes

My father was born in 1882. He was the fourth child in a family of five. His father, Helton Baynes, owned a timber firm in Reading and they lived their lives with the austerity that was typical at the time within a very devout Quaker family.

Godwin was sent to Layton Park, a Quaker school in Reading. After school, he served his apprenticeship in his father's timber firm, Gabriel Wade and English. His mother, Mary, a large and generous person, was related, through her mother's side of the family, to the original thinker and political philosopher, William Godwin, which is why my father was christened Godwin. Both his parents were unusually tall; their three sons were all over 6'; my father, at 6'4 1/2", was the shortest of the three brothers. His two sisters were also over 6'.

Godwin rebelled against the strict puritan values of his parents. He was deeply affected by his father's problem with agoraphobia, making it impossible for Helton to go outside without an umbrella. To prove that he hadn't inherited his father's neurosis, Godwin would make a point of climbing the tallest trees in their garden whenever his father was around.

Godwin's parents were close friends with another Quaker family, the parents of the composer, Sir Arnold Bax.

Mrs Bax took a liking to Godwin and agreed to finance his medical studies at Cambridge, on condition that he spent a year after he qualified working among the poor. Godwin found the freedom and wider possibilities he discovered in Cambridge exhilarating and became part of two very different groups. He was one of the young men who devoted their time to athletics, winning both a swimming and a rowing blue, but he also belonged to the avant-garde group of poets, writers and artists who surrounded Rupert Brooke; this included the poet and the Plato scholar, Frances and Francis Cornford, as well as the artists, Jacques and Gwen Raverat.

When Godwin arrived in London to continue his medical studies at St Bartholomew's, he spent his free time at the spacious Hampstead house of the Bax family. Among the musicians, poets and writers who were a part of this circle were Arnold and Clifford Bax, Eleanor Farjeon, David Garnet, Rupert Brooke, Edward Thomas, Myra Hess, D.H. Lawrence and many others. They dispensed with all Victorian conventions; for my father, it symbolized a final rejection of all the puritan restrictions of his upbringing. He fell in love with Rosalind Thorneycroft, daughter of the royal academician, Sir Hamo Thorneycroft, and, most unusually for the time, (1910), they lived together before they were married while he was working in his first practice in Bethnal Green. Rosalind managed the dispensary and Godwin's younger sister, Ruth, acted as chaperone.

Godwin and Rosalind had an unconventional wedding in a church in Ireland and rode away from the church on bicycles for a romantic honeymoon in Derry. Their first daughter, Bridget, was born when Godwin and Rosalind had moved to Wisbech, where Godwin became the first panel doctor, in 1912. Bridget was delivered by my father in 1914, just before the outbreak of the First World War. By 1916, he felt he could no longer remain in England when doctors were needed to attend to the wounded in France, so he left his family shortly before the birth of his second daughter, Chloe. It was devastating for Rosalind to be left with two tiny children and without help, particularly when it was not necessary for Godwin, as a doctor, to go to the Western Front.

Cracks had begun to appear in their marriage and when Godwin returned from the war, having served as a doctor in both France and Mesopotamia, he found Rosalind had given birth to another daughter by someone else and she wanted a divorce. It was a bleak homecoming for Godwin. In his sister Ruth's words, he was, at the time, 'shipwrecked'. He was so traumatized by his experiences during the war and his own near-death experience when he was wounded in France, that he was no longer the wildly extraverted young man of his student days. He became interested in the whole new concept of 'shell shock', the psychological aspects of trauma, which today would be referred to as post-traumatic stress disorder (PTSD). He was thus beginning to turn his attention to psychiatry, which was, at the time, a relatively new branch of medicine.

While working at The Maudsley Hospital in London, Godwin came across the work of C.G. Jung and subsequently visited him at his home in Küsnacht, near Zurich. From that moment, his life changed. He discovered something in the work of Jung that affected him profoundly and he devoted his whole life to understanding this introverted way of being, which was so very different from the overwhelming extraversion of his life up to that point. He decided to study with Jung in order to become a Jungian analyst; before long he was working as Jung's assistant in Zurich and translating Jung's early works into English.

In 1922, he became one of the first Jungian analysts in London, where he founded the Jung Club, known as the APC (Analytical Psychology Club), which is still thriving today.

Godwin had three further marriages, first to Hilda Davidson, a beautiful young–woman and also a concert pianist, with whom he had a son, Christopher. Hilda suffered from depression and very sadly she took her life in 1925, when Christopher was only two, on the eve of Godwin's departure with Jung to East Africa. The purpose of their trip was to study the dreams of the Elgonyi people, who at the time had had almost no contact with the outside world. On his return from Africa, Godwin, (who, since working with Jung, had become known to everyone as Peter) married Cary de Angelou, a colleague of Jung, who was also involved in the translation of Jung's books. She had a young daughter called Ximena. This marriage was short-lived, perhaps because my father met my mother, Agnes Leay, an exceptionally beautiful young woman in her twenties, with whom he fell in love.

The years of my father's marriage to Anne, (as she became known), were the happiest, and also the most creative, period of his life. However, it was interrupted by the outbreak of WWII and was short-lived. Peter and Anne had three children together: Michael, John and Diana. He built up a practice in London as well as in the beautiful home they created in Surrey. Having worked as Jung's assistant in Zurich for many years, Peter then distanced himself from Jung's powerful influence. As a result, he was able to create his own Jungian world in London.

Peter wrote three books on Jungian psychology, which have become Jungian classics.

He died in 1943 of a brain tumour, leaving a widow, three small children and three older ones.

Agnes Sarah Leay

I know little about my mother's parents. My mother's father, Frederick Leay, was an orphan. He must have been exceptionally bright. I believe that he excelled at school and eventually had a very successful career as a vice consul general.

Agnes's mother, Laura Higginson, was born in 1867. She came from an aristocratic family and among her forebears there was certainly an Admiral and possibly a General. Raised in a conventional family, Laura was brought up to be 'a lady', which meant that she was entirely helpless when it came to any practical task. Her husband's job took them to Panama, Mexico and Valparaíso, where they lived in palatial and fully staffed houses.

Laura Higginson was the youngest of five children: Edith and Maude were her older sisters, followed by Percy – for whom my mother had a particular fondness – then Cecil. Laura's early life was spent developing the accomplishments suitable for a young lady and those that were required, also, to 'win' a husband. Frederick Leay was introduced to the family as an eligible bachelor. He fell in love with Laura, a gentle and beautiful young woman. Laura's parents, Sarah and James Pickford Higginson, told Frederick he could marry Laura's older sister, Maude. It wasn't considered right for a younger sister to marry before her older sisters. However, Frederick was determined to marry Laura and so eventually, Laura's parents had to consent to the match. Laura and Frederick married in 1892.

My mother, Agnes, was Laura's fourth child; she was born in 1903. She had no permanent home during childhood due to her father's job. Born in Mexico, my mother always maintained that she flourished because she was breastfed, in contrast to her siblings, as there was no artificial food in Mexico with which to feed babies. My mother's two older brothers, both healthy full-term babies, were born in Panama and died soon after birth, due to ignorance and mismanagement. Her sister, Freda, who was four years older than my mother, was a sickly child who became mentally ill with catatonic schizophrenia. She was sent to an asylum at the age of eighteen, from which she never returned home.

My mother spoke of a lack of physical warmth from

both her parents. There was little affection, also, from Miss Armour, the governess who dominated my mother and her sister Freda's childhood. As her name suggests, she was rigid in her approach to the children's upbringing and Miss Armour's main pre-occupation was to ensure her charges should 'be good'. My mother remembered their time in America, where they lived close to the Adirondack Mountains, as the happiest period in her childhood. She went to a liberal school, called, most appropriately, 'New Hope'. Here she experienced real happiness and freedom for the first time.

Her parents' marriage became increasingly stressful. Frederick suffered from paranoia and repeatedly accused his loyal and gentle wife of infidelity and embezzlement. Finally, it became too much for Laura and they agreed to separate when Agnes was 19. Frederick's condition became intolerable and he was committed to an asylum. My mother despised her father and he knew this to be so. He would quote Shakespeare's King Lear to her, 'How sharper than a serpent's tooth it is to have a thankless child.'

My mother grew to be exceptionally beautiful: slender and graceful with ash blonde hair. Many men wanted to marry her; due to her family's trauma, however, she initially felt unable to marry. She trained as a secretary and worked for several years in London, including a stint as political secretary to Nancy Astor, the first woman M.P. As a result, she was rubbing shoulders with women who were supporting the women's suffrage movement. However, my mother was not particularly interested in women gaining political power; her ambitions were much humbler. She simply wanted to stay sane, marry and have children!

When she was 26, my mother was invited by one of her admirers to stay at Admiralty House in Malta. The young man wanted to marry Agnes, but she felt unable to accept his proposal. She returned from Malta – having been fêted and adored and, perhaps, feeling temporarily freed from her family's difficulties - to find that her mother had committed suicide. Laura had suffered for some time from depression and was aware of becoming a burden to her daughter. She had taken an overdose of sleeping pills. My mother found a note beside her bed, 'Am so sorry to cause you trouble, am quite helpless. Goodbye darling Agnes, don't grieve. Am happier so.

The death of her beloved mother hit my mother like a body blow. She also felt guilty that while she was having the time of her life, her mother's despair had become intolerable. The separation from her husband after years of accusations against her, in addition to the loss of three of her four children, had all become too much for Laura. My mother returned from Malta to discover that she was now entirely on her own.

Agnes remained alienated from her father, who she blamed for her mother's unhappiness and suicide. Eventually, Frederick recovered sufficiently to be released from the asylum and he was able to marry a woman called Margaret with whom he had a daughter, Petra. In later life, there was a rapprochement between Frederick and my mother. She maintained contact with both Margaret and Petra and we, too, were able to meet them.

My mother spoke of herself at this time in her life as, 'a rolling stone that gathers no moss.' She saw herself as outwardly confident but inwardly lost. She was also terrified that she too would suffer from some kind of mental illness. When my parents met, there was an immediate sense of empathy, perhaps as a result of the traumas they had both endured.

My mother maintained that if she had not met Peter, with his maturity, psychological understanding and wisdom, she would never have been able to marry.

My parent's marriage only lasted twelve years, but it was deeply fulfilling and enabling.

It was a time of extraordinary happiness for them both.

Laura and
Frederick Leay

Part One

Chapter 1

In the Beginning

All the world's a stage, and all the men and women merely players; they have their exits and their entrances, and one man in his time plays many parts, his act being seven ages. At first the infant, mewling and puking in the nurse's arms.

(Shakespeare: *As You Like It*, 1.iv)

It is a spring morning and I am a small girl, hidden among a forest of rhododendrons.

The garden is a green wilderness. In the woodland we are making small houses of mud beside the big beech tree that forms part of our boundary. One of the roots of the tree forms a strange, knotted shape. We have called this root our seal. The houses of the village span out from these roots and become a place that belongs to us. I forget who I am with or what age I might be; I only remember clearly the sensation of a spring morning, the world aglow, birds singing, sun filtering through the new beech leaves and our world hidden from view by a bank of tall rhododendrons. A secret world, unknown and unseen by the grown-ups, in which we could live our days of magic and imagination undisturbed.

The entrance to this hidden garden among the rhododendrons was where my father, at an earlier time, had shown me a cluster of grass snake's eggs resting on a large pile of leaves. They were white and were strung together in a single mass, like frog's spawn. Later, we watched them as the tiny green snakes emerged, perfectly formed, from each fragile white receptacle. The miracle of life as it transforms from its static to its vital form: life in all its variety and wonder. That sense of newness and surprise is in my life again today.

Diana and her donkey

There are moments that come back to me, often triggered by a scent or a sensation. For instance, while I was staying with my daughter and son-in-law, Cathy and Roman and their small son, Fynn, in Botswana, I would spend every afternoon lying under the great fig tree in their camp. In the tree there was every kind of bird: parrots and hornbills, rollers, bee-eaters and kingfishers. Little squirrel-like animals leapt from branch to branch, enjoying the ripe fruit. The wind shook the leaves and the sun filtered through the thick leafy canopy. As I lay there, enjoying the tree's noisy and ceaseless activity, free of all care and concerns, I was once more a small child.

I remembered vividly the feeling - an almost blissful sensation - of lying in my pram under the large oak tree, which grew on the lawn outside my father's study. It was a summer's afternoon; I remember sensing the gentle rocking motion of the old carriage pram in the wind and seeing patches of blue sky through the leaves that rustled above me. At that time of year the birds were busy feeding their young, and I remember the various songs; perhaps of blackbirds, thrushes and robins, of wrens, chaffinches and dunnocks.

I was suddenly startled by a small bird landing on the side of my pram and by its sense of panic at being pursued, probably by a sparrow hawk. Maybe it was something that was different from my everyday experience of sleeping in that pram, which has made it memorable. Perhaps, also, it was the contrast between my own sense of security and contentment and the small bird's panic. I recalled some of the sensations of that early experience in my pram as I swung in the tree hammock in Botswana, surrounded by the natural world with no man-made sound to interrupt the absolute tranquillity of the place.

Diana on Reed House lawn

I was born at home at Reed House in West Byfleet, Surrey, on June 5th, 1937, at 11.21 pm. I was my mother's third child, so the birth was quick and uncomplicated, and I was born at home at Reed House in West Byfleet, Surrey, on June 5th, 1937, at 11.21 pm. My mother had longed for a daughter and told me that her first words on discovering that I was a girl, were, 'now I am the happiest woman in the world.' So, I arrived to a great welcome!

Anne with Diana

My father, a Jungian analyst, had a friend and colleague called Eva Metman, who was an astrologer. My father asked her to do my horoscope soon after I was born; the beginning reads, 'This will be an

extremely lovable and loving child. Very womanly and receptive, warm-blooded and affectionate, free from vice and all evil intent, combining the powerful forces of natural growth, the conserving tendencies of a deep-rooted tree, with a lofty, graceful and imaginative mind that floats over the world like a summer breeze over a flowering meadow.'
Is it really possible to tell so much about a person from the very beginning? Anyway, the predictions about marrying twice and turning to further education later in life, have both, astonishingly, turned out to be correct!

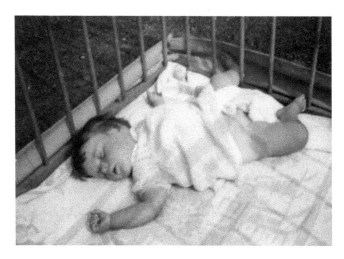

Diana, aged 6 months

In January of that year we suffered a cataclysmic event. Reed House, with its thatched roof and old-world charm, which my parents had bought five years earlier, was burned to the ground. It happened on a bitterly cold January day. My mother was in bed with a cold. The maid went out to hang the clothes on the washing line and noticed a shower of sparks rising from the thatch above my mother's bedroom. Fire engines were summoned but it was already too late and the house went up in flames.

The family moved to Clare Cottage, a rented house in Pyford, while a more modern house was built on the foundations of the old. My father built a typical 1930's house, which was light and had generous proportions, but did not possess the cosiness of the old house. The building works took about a year. Our new house had nine bedrooms, very large reception rooms, servants' quarters and a separate area for the children and nannies. The rooms downstairs all had French windows that led into the large and beautiful garden. It is this house that I remember well and it is here that I spent all the days of my childhood.

The pervading sense I have of my early childhood is of long summer days and the freedom of a large garden in which to play. There was the companionship of my two older brothers who were mostly kind but could often reduce me to tears. It was in the days of nannies: we had our part of the house and the grown-ups kept to theirs. Our parents were often with us in the nursery, but it was our nanny, and later our governess, who shared our meals, dressed us in the morning and put us to bed. Rosaline is the nanny I remember. She had shoulder-length brown hair and rather fat legs and she was much more interested in the soldiers stationed down the road than she was in us children.

Our parents were quite often away but that didn't seem to affect us; the routine of the nursery continued so there was security in the absolute regularity of this. Nothing changed. Rosaline dressed me at the same time every morning. I remember making her laugh as she enveloped me in the layers of viyella clothing necessary to keep warm in winter in a house which had very little heating, and struggling to say the word 'petticoat'. I repeated the word over and over - 'pecitot, pecitot,' - and couldn't understand why she was so amused. Our breakfast was brought to the nursery and I would sit at the table in my high chair. Then it was time for my brothers to get ready for school while I sat with Rosaline at the nursery table to do 'lessons', until it was time to go outside.

Mickey, John and Diana

My mother and father were comparatively distant figures in the very early years. However, I do remember a scene with my parents on a sunny summer's day; I was perhaps 2 or 3 years old.

I was sitting on the wide stone steps that led down to the long walk and my father's prized herbaceous border. I was sobbing inconsolably and both my parents, who were sitting at the garden table nearby, were laughing. I have totally forgotten the reason for my tears. I only remember how it felt to have my misery so disregarded and to feel ridiculed by them. I must have been in a sulk; perhaps there had been a 'no' to some unreasonable request of mine. I recall my misery was not about the thing that had caused my tears but the shame and sense of ridicule I felt as a result of their laughter. I believe children are especially sensitive to ridicule, which is intensified if they have no idea what has caused the laughter. It is quite possible that my parents were laughing at the intensity of my passion or at a certain degree of play-acting, but my enduring sense was one of humiliation.

There were daily walks. I remember one in particular: I am warmly dressed and sitting upright in my large carriage pram, being pushed by Rosaline. My two brothers are walking on either side of her. It is autumn, leaves are falling; there is a sprinkling of oak leaves across the narrow avenue where we live. I can observe everything from my position in the pram and feel a certain sense of advantage over my brothers, who are walking reluctantly.

Our nanny, Rosaline, is also our governess. I don't remember feeling any real warmth from her and have no sense of her as an important figure in my childhood. She is simply there. She does the things she has to do for us; bathing and dressing me and overseeing my brothers, presiding over our nursery meals, correcting our manners and accompanying us on our mandatory afternoon walks.

I remember the slow meandering progress along the road. The traffic is so infrequent we have no need to stay on the pavement. My brothers are running ahead, shouting as they race and laugh and play tag with one another. Then we reach the end of Old Avenue where it joins the main road, Sheerwater Road. They are brought to heel and told to hold onto the pram as we walk along the wide pavement. An occasional car passes by. Then we arrive at the railway bridge, from where we can watch the steam trains as they pass beneath us.

This is where my brothers love to be, enjoying the intense excitement created by the sound of a distant train. The first billow of smoke and the steadily building sound as the train approaches us, - ch chudely ch chudely ch – 'til, with a burst of steam and a thrilling roar, it passes like a mighty dragon right under the bridge where we stand. The excitement never diminishes; for my brothers, it is perhaps their first experience of an absolute, terrifying - yet also wonderful - sense of power, with which they long to identify. At this stage, like so many other boys of their age, they both want to become engine drivers; later, they would both fall in love with the internal combustion engine, in all its ramifications.

After the fifth or sixth train has passed, it is time to leave. Our next stop is the soldiers' camp a little further along the road. This is where Rosaline meets another nanny and from where they watch the soldiers come and go, exchanging a few bashful words with one or two. We are well aware that this is the place our nanny really wants to be. The other nanny has a charge called Rosemary, a pretty child who is always decked out in ribbons and bows and elaborate frocks. Her nanny is more severe than ours; if Rosemary does something to displease her, the nanny shouts at her in a shrill voice; 'If you do that again I will take you into the middle of the road and take down your knickers and spank you.' We rather hoped she would, but it never happened!

I'm sure this walk was a daily occurrence, probably in all weathers; the clockwork routine of children's lives in those days never varied. However, it is this one day that stands out in my memory. It is the mixture of the known and familiar, the security and ordinariness of a daily event coupled with the unexpected: the thrill, excitement and sense of possibility in what might be about to happen. How new and exciting life is to a child. Nothing has yet become ordinary or boring. All the little things that make up a day are filled with magic and wonder. Perhaps today we try to entertain children too much, providing entertainment and stimulation when life itself is all the stimulation that a child requires.

After the walk we return to a blazing fire in the nursery grate. Our toys are kept in large wall cupboards with old oak doors. We have a shelf each, though Mickey has a cupboard all to himself that is always known as the 'Christmas Cupboard'. We play with our toys by the fire while nanny makes tea. This is usually the time of day when our mother comes to the nursery to join in our games. Daddy always comes later, when he has finished seeing patients.

* * *

These memories conjure up a time of stability; a time when the world was a safe place. Our daily routine gave us, perhaps, a sense that the world could be depended upon; lunch was always at one o'clock and teatime at four. Not even a war could alter these things. We had our rituals each day and between these certainties we had the freedom of a large garden, where we could play unsupervised; naked in the summer, buttoned up in winter, but with a sense that the world was ours.

When I was 2 years old, WW11 was declared. I have a dim memory of something important and disturbing occurring the day war was announced on the radio, without understanding what it was. But during the course of 1939, and perhaps until the end of 1940, when the phoney war was over, the fact that we were at war had little impact on our lives.

In 1941, when I was 4 years old, we had a holiday in Devon. It is the first holiday I remember and was also the last we took for many years. Travelling became increasingly difficult during the war years. We boarded the train at Paddington and were met by a taxi at Exeter St. David's station. The taxi took us to our destination: the small village of Bantham.

It may be my first train journey. How exciting it feels to be picnicking in our carriage, gazing out at the changing scenes from the window; towns, villages, pastures with cows and sheep, people and cyclists and motor-cars. And then comes the first view of the sea; long strands of perfect sand with children and adults playing, their heads bobbing in the shallow water and the sea stretching with its splendour of azure blue to a horizon that reaches to the infinity of heaven.

Our arrival at our destination is traumatic. I have managed to catch my index finger in the hinge of the taxi door. It comes out quite flattened. At first I am too shocked to react, or even to feel the pain. Then, quite suddenly, it is an all-consuming pain that simply can't be managed. Tears are no relief. My father picks me up, holds me, comforts me and then attends to the damaged finger. Did we go to hospital or to a doctor? I don't remember. But it heals well and in no way diminishes the pleasures of the holiday.

There is a village street and a row of terraced houses, of which our lodging house is one. Opposite the house is the pub and I can hear the noise of laughter and broad West-Country accents floating up to me in the summer evenings as I lie in my cot under the window. I remember the warm scents and the voices and strangeness of it all. Perhaps it is the first time I've been aware of sleeping anywhere that isn't home. It feels exciting and as though we are a part of an unfamiliar world. I have a feeling of absolute well-being and contentment.

The impressions are vivid; walking with my father over the fields near to our pension to gather wild mushrooms for our breakfast. He wakes me, helps me to dress and we then climb the nearby hill, walking together through the damp grass studded with a multitude of wild flowers: clover, cornflowers, buttercups and poppies. For me it is an enchanted flower garden. Among the meadow grass and wild flowers are the caps of the mushrooms, each one a perfect white dome. Carefully, we pull each mushroom without damaging its perfection and gently place it in our basket. Then, holding my father's hand, we return to present our landlady with our breakfast.

Such lovely scents and sounds on that long-ago morning and how fresh and new it all was, with shimmering webs strung between the long grasses. I remember my father's huge presence and the wonder of having him entirely to myself - perhaps this is why the memory stands out from all others. It was a rare event indeed in such difficult wartime conditions. It is as though all early mornings and walks over meadows and gathering of wild mushrooms and the sounds, scents and delights that accompany them are like a reflection of that first time when all the world seemed new.

Every day our family, together with Rosaline, walk the mile or two to the beach. I find it exhausting trying to keep up with my father's long strides and my brothers, who race on ahead. In the end, after much persuading from me, my father, who is 6'41/2'', hoists me up onto his broad shoulders and I gain a new perspective on life as I look down on the world and my two brothers from my magnificent seven-foot tall perch.

By the age of four I become much more aware. I have no recollection however, of the holiday we took the year before, at Corfe Castle. It is possible that I wasn't even there and had stayed behind with our Nanny because I was too small. I remember my brothers talking about this holiday, but I had no memory of it and felt as if I had somehow missed out.

It must be the same summer. I am four or five years old and playing on the big lawn in the garden at Reed House. It is a warm summer's day, but that was so for all my childhood summers. Was the sun always shining? My brother, John, is with me. Perhaps we are playing Cowboys and Indians. He has a bow and arrow. It was probably a recent birthday present. He is the Indian and I am no doubt the enemy. Suddenly, I feel a searing pain just above my left eye. It is an excellent shot; John has struck a bulls-eye on the enemy target. My screams bring my mother running to the garden. Blood is pouring down my face. I am taken to our local GP, Dr Bilby, to have the wound stitched.

John could be a rascal, but an entirely loveable rascal.

He needed to test all the boundaries, particularly with my father. There is another memory. I am perhaps two or three. It is early in the morning when my father comes storming into the nursery with John, a screaming small boy, tucked under one arm. I have never seen my father in such a tearing rage. It feels as though a mighty hurricane has burst into the quiet un-eventfulness of our nursery existence, although I am unaware as to what has given rise to his rage. Only later I discover from John that he had the ingenious idea of parking his little red wooden engine behind my father's Studebaker, so that when my father reverses up the drive on his way to work he will, unbeknown to him, be pushing John to the top of the drive and saving his son from the effort of pedalling. And having reached the top of this slight incline, John will have the fun of freewheeling all the way down to the garage.

It is only when my father feels the impact with the little engine and the crunch of smashed wood that he realizes he has struck an obstacle and has nearly run over his little son. That must have been the first of my brother's nine lives and the beginning of his delight in taking risks with anything that had wheels!

These moments of both profound joy but also, at times, total abject misery, return with all their intensity as I write. Perhaps I absorbed in some way the great pleasure my father took in his garden and the sense of peace and equanimity it brought him. He would say that in his work as an analytical psychologist he needed to give so much of himself. Patients needed a verbal response, whereas the plants and flowers in his garden grew by themselves. Best of all, they couldn't talk! It is possible that my passion for gardening now and the delight I derive from the plants in my garden have their origins in those long summer days when walking alongside my father, I fill my tiny wheelbarrow with weeds. I follow my father down the long walk and help him weed the herbaceous border lying to the right; in summer it is a riot of colour with plants much taller than me. To the left of the long walk, growing close to the great bank of rhododendrons that form the Western border of our garden, is a shrubbery with a variety of different greens and colours that come and go according to the time of year. At the bottom of the garden is a round bed; it may have roses in it. If you walk beyond the cultivated garden, you then arrive at a woodland area where many varieties of rhododendrons grow. Here, the children play hide and seek and swing from the roof of the cedar wood summer house, holding on to the tall bamboo stems which grow there, landing gently on the woodland floor below. This is my favourite part of the garden. In the bottom left hand corner there is a small gate that leads into the beech woods beyond. This is where we love to play and build houses from bracken. In our childish minds it is a place of danger and adventure beyond the safety of our four and a half acre garden.

Sometimes we walk through the woods with our father to a heath-like area beyond the trees, where he practices throwing his boomerang. It seems quite impossible, the way this sickle-shaped piece of wood can sweep round describing a huge circle and arrive back again in his hand. While he is pretending to be in the Australian outback my brothers and I pick up small slivers of silver paper dropped by German planes to confuse the British radar system. These are known as 'windows'. Sometimes, also, we discover small kaki tin boxes known as K rations, which contain delicious things such as chocolate and biscuits and possibly bully beef. I don't know why these have been dropped in our woods, but it is a source of great excitement whenever we discover one.

Childhood is a time of intense feelings. The feelings overwhelm but there are no words yet to frame them. Although my memories of those early days of childhood are mostly happy, I do have a single recollection of complete and total abandonment. Although the experience is brief and no such thing ever happened again, the incident gives me an understanding of the child whose life is abusive. I am possibly 3 or 4 at the time of this punishment; it occurs while my nanny and I are still sleeping together in the room we call the night nursery. Perhaps I have been naughty, though I have no memory of what I have done. I am taken to the night nursery and locked into the room. My fear is that this imprisonment will last forever. Never again will I see my parents and gradually I will starve to death. No one has told me that the punishment will end. An hour, to a small child, can feel like eternity. I am battering on the door, crying and shouting and then eventually, as no one comes, I sit quietly on the bed and consider the possibility of jumping from the window. There is, I suppose, the accompanying thought, 'and then they'll be sorry.' I suppose that shutting a child in his or her room after a warning or two is a normal enough punishment, but I think the difference for me was the terror of being *locked* in, having no escape route and not knowing whether I would ever again be free.

My parents possibly heard about this punishment and remonstrated with our nanny, because it was never repeated. The event dates from the time when we still had both a governess and a nanny and we lived lives that were essentially quite separate from our parents. This period was short-lived. Soon after the war began in 1939 it became difficult to find people to employ as everyone was involved in the war effort in some way or other.

Another memory: the war has begun, although it is perhaps still the phoney war. There is no longer any employed help in the house. My parents have left with John to visit Mickey at Port Regis, his prep school in Dorset, for half term. I am left behind at home in the care of my godmother, Evie D'Oyly, known to us as Midiboo. I have a lovely time, with all the loving attention any little girl could hope for. She is unused to small children and is at times confused with the number of simultaneous events that occur in a normal household. She invents a little song with words that go something like this; 'Kettle boiling, telephone ringing, dog barking, doorbell ringing, toast burning and Dinny crying'. She finds herself running to and fro attending to all these demands, whereas at home her maid would attend to everything.

An extraordinarily beautiful woman, Midiboo is probably already well into her sixties with perfectly coiffured pure white hair, intensely blue eyes, a slim figure and erect posture. She is always exquisitely dressed and wears a ring with a large blue stone on her left hand; I notice that the blue of the stone exactly matches the blue of her eyes. I love being with her and we spend the time playing cards and making up guessing games together. It is a happy time. I don't remember missing my parents. They arrive home after I am settled in my cot. By this time, my yellow cot has been moved into my parent's bedroom. My father comes up to see me. He brings me a present. It is a little book; Beatrix Potter's *Johnny Town Mouse.* However, I have no intention of greeting him or of enjoying my present. They left me behind and they are going to be punished. So, I refuse to look at my father or to speak to him. None of his most tender cajoling or repeated enquiries about my time with Midiboo can woo me from my sulk. Surely, they must know I'd had a horrid time at home without them? How could they go away without me, especially as John had been allowed to accompany them?

How long I manage to hold out is difficult to say; to ignore my father takes some doing! I am so keenly aware of the sense of betrayal and of the feeling that I never want to speak to them again.

I experienced this again with my own little children. Coming home after a short absence, excited at the prospect of seeing the child again, only to be left ignored and un-greeted as the tiny child expresses his or her displeasure at being left behind. 'You didn't want me and now I don't want you ... so there'.

How powerfully I remember that feeling!

* * *

Christmases

Perhaps we re-live the magic and excitement of childhood Christmases with our own children and now with grandchildren. It feels, with each Christmas, as though I am re-living all the others. Each day is an expanded time of wonder and enjoyment of little things: the lights and the Christmas tree, the pleasure of wrapping parcels and of singing carols. The voices, cards, re-connecting with old friends; memories cluster around all these happenings and lend them a touch of wonder. I am a child again.

I remember Christmas when I was three and the thrill of finding a stocking full of small parcels with Red Indians and a spinning top. I remember the excitement of having Christmas lunch in the dining room with the grown-ups and also with my grown-up half-brother Christopher. It is served by the cook in the dining room, instead of by our nanny in the nursery. Christmas lunch is a rare feast of roast chicken, which is not easy to come by on war-time rations. I sit beside my father in my high chair. Later, we open parcels in our large drawing room, the stove burning merrily in the newly refurbished grate surrounded by old Dutch tiles, each one depicting a different scene. My present is a large, wooden Noah's ark filled with wooden animals. The ark's sloping green roof opens on one side and the beautifully hand-carved animals - the males slightly different from the females - can be taken out. I remember the smell and texture of these animals and my pride in the possession of something so beautiful.

By the Christmas of 1941, war is in full swing. The house is filled with friends from London seeking sanctuary from the London bombing. I have asked Father Christmas for a torch but when I open my stocking on Christmas morning, with my father watching from his bed, there is no torch! My father sees my disappointment and comments, 'could Father Christmas have dropped it on his way down the chimney?' I leap out of my cot and carefully examine the small fireplace that is built into the main wall of my parent's bedroom. There it is, among the soot, a beautiful silver torch. No present has ever felt so magical and so important. My father roars with laughter at my delight and it doesn't occur to me to wonder how a portly Father Christmas could have squeezed his way down that narrow chimney.

That Christmas was when the world was still whole and my trust in the certainty of things had not been broken. We were still a complete family and Christmases were proof that all was well with the world. Older members of the family joined us; we played games and sang around the piano. Such times - when generations gathered together to enjoy laughter and light-hearted games - were rare. It was almost as if we were not being bombed every night.

The following Christmas my present from my father is an upright, Victorian school desk that is dark brown and stained with ink. I have asked for a desk at which to write my first book at the age of 6, imagining a tiny coloured child's desk similar to the one belonging to my friend. But this tall, dark, grown up desk is a terrible disappointment. I don't know how much my disappointment shows but I never become fond of it. And it doesn't have a good karma! I can feel in its aura the agonies of generations of Victorian school children as they struggle to become literate and numerate! That Christmas evening my parents give a party. Friends arrive and my father's adopted daughter – a comely young woman called Nan - visits from London. Someone plays the piano while she sings operatic arias in a thin, reedy voice. Everyone claps loudly while I long for her to stop.

The next day it snows. It is deep, soft snow and our garden is transformed into a new, unfamiliar place. We toboggan down our sloping drive and go to a nearby hill where my father holds me in front of him - his great arms securing me as I place my feet on top of his - while he skis down what seem to me to be terrifyingly steep and dangerous slopes, the snow flying from under his skis. I remember the feel of the snow and the sense of acceleration as we speed downwards. At the same time, I am aware of the sense of absolute safety knowing that my father is holding me.

The year after, how different things are! My mother is mortally ill in hospital with septicaemia; the doctor does not hold out much hope for her survival. My father also is ill but no one is yet aware of this. He is overwhelmed by his responsibilities: a family of three young children and three other children from previous marriages who need money for their education. Brigit, in her twenties, is at Art College. Chloe, her younger sister, is at university and Christopher, at seventeen, is still at public school. Expenses are mounting, inflation is rising and investments have suddenly dwindled in the stock market crash. My father is over-worked; most of his Jungian analyst colleagues have been called up. He is finding it increasingly difficult to speak and is burdened with crushing anxiety and tiredness.

Our brother Christopher has been entrusted with the task of delivering our stockings. We three younger children are sleeping together in our parent's room. Mickey, aged ten, and Johnny, now eight, have already awakened. They wake me too. There, at the end of our beds are our still empty stockings. Then comes the sound of heavy footsteps on the landing. We all pretend to be asleep. In walks Miss Mack, our lady gardener, in her Wellington boots. It is 6.00 am and the rest of the household is still sleeping. Christopher has overslept and Miss Mack has found the filled stockings outside his room. She leaves the room, noisily, and we are left to open our stockings together, any lingering belief in Father Christmas shattered forever!

That was the end of Christmas magic, until I had my own children. They brought back the excitement, the wonder and the belief that life could still be trusted and that the world could still be a place of wonder. The carols, tree decorating and Father Christmas magic. The stockings that were brought into our room at 5 o'clock in the morning, each little parcel a treasure to be enjoyed at leisure. The offerings for Father Christmas left on the window sill: nuts, a tangerine and a bottle of Newcastle Brown Ale. Only the shells, the peel and the empty bottle were proof that he really had been.

Why does the magic so often disappear from adult life? Is it when we think we know all the answers and no longer believe that 'all shall be well and all shall be well and all manner of thing shall be well'? How sad it is when we are too busy, too pre-occupied, to feel the wonder of a frosty morning; when spiders' webs become wondrous works of art, their tiny silken mandalas hanging from hedges, etched with frost; when trees become feathered with a lacework of frosted white against an ice blue sky; when the first snowdrops peep through the brown leaf-strewn woodland floor bringing once again the promise of new life. Their emergence is a little spring of hope long before spring becomes any kind of reality in our northern wind-swept home.

These are wonders that bring with them every year a new faith that life, however precarious, can and will renew itself. This profound faith in the possibility of life's renewal, is it solely from the sense of having, as a tiny child, experienced being so absolutely and profoundly held?

Held in a mother's steadfast and life-long love and in the strong arms of a father who for me, was so briefly and yet so magnificently present.

Reed House

Chapter 2

Another Era

Once more unto the breach, dear friends, once more; or close the wall up with our English dead. In peace, there's nothing so becomes a man as modest stillness, and humility: But when the blast of war blows in our ears, then imitate the action of a tiger...
(Shakespeare: Henry V, Act 3.ii)

As the war years progressed my mother, who had never before needed to cook or attend to the practical tasks of housekeeping, suddenly found herself without help and with an enormous household for which to cook and wash. We may have had a hoover but there were certainly no dishwashers or washing machines in the 1940s. She attempted to maintain the same standard of comfort as in the days of the cook and house-parlour maid. She rose at dawn to make a fire in the dining room so the family and the many guests (these included the Jungian analyst, Eddie Bennet, and his wife Floey, another of my three godmothers, and their family), who stayed with us to avoid the London bombings, could enjoy comparative warmth at breakfast time. Breakfast was the usual bacon and eggs served on the sideboard under a silver canopy. And so it continued throughout the day; three cooked meals and every comfort besides. Of course, the guests didn't think of helping because it had never before occurred to them or been necessary.

I remember one morning in particular. I am sleeping in my yellow cot in my parent's bedroom (Rosaline is no longer with us and the last of our helpers has disappeared). The alarm clock goes off and my mother misreads the time. She gets up, lights the fire and cooks the breakfast – but no one appears. It is then that she discovers it is only 4.00am, not 8.00am as she had thought. My parents are helpless with laughter at her mistake. But behind the laughter is also a sense of anxiety and exhaustion, and it is of this feeling that I am aware.

Soon afterwards my mother becomes ill. For six months or more she battles against an infection that begins in her toe and develops into septicaemia, from which she almost dies. Doctors tell her she needs to have her left leg amputated but she refuses to endure this mutilation. Penicillin has by this time been discovered but is only available for the troops. However, the sulphonamide drugs are in the early stages of being available to the general public and it is the sulphonamide drug, M&B, that eventually saves my mother's life.

My mother's leg remained swollen and disfigured for the rest of her life but at least she didn't lose it. She had an amazingly strong will and a desire to live that seemed to overcome all the predictions that she wouldn't survive; she maintained it was because of her children and her need to live for them. She returned home from the Weybridge hospital in August 1943, two months after her fortieth birthday. She was still on crutches and very much a convalescent.

My father employed a woman called Mrs. Bennett to look after us in my mother's absence. She arrived one day with Midiboo, who had contacted her, and they entered together through the kitchen door. I was watching from the other side of the room. Mrs Bennet looked at me and said, with a ghastly false smile, 'I simply leeerve children.' I said to myself, 'Oh no you do not!' With the ability of a young child to discern what is real, I knew this woman was lying through her teeth. Indeed, she turned out to be impossible in every way, but she did at least keep us fed and out of trouble. I have few memories of her.

I remember one evening, for no apparent reason, she comes storming into my room while I am in my cot in the little bedroom at the top of the back stairs (which had, at one time belonged to our cook), and beats me; I believe it was because I hadn't said my prayers. She is also dishonest and steals all my mother's precious provisions of wartime food - tins that are being saved in her store cupboard for a rainy day. We discover that she is also stealing all our butter rations. My father is too preoccupied and exhausted to be aware of what is happening.

The cruellest thing of all for me is the time when she prevents me from going to the Weybridge hospital on one of the rare occasions when we were allowed to visit our mother. It is a hot June day. I have been playing barefoot in the road at the top of our driveway. It is a quiet cul-de-sac and during the war years, when only doctors have an allowance for petrol, there is no traffic. The tar on the road has begun to melt due to the heat. It oozes in-between my toes in a delicious black, warm squelch. I run home for lunch, prepared by Mrs. Bennet. She sees my tarry feet and is furious. She says that unless we are able to remove the tar before the afternoon she will not allow me to visit my mother. For an hour or more I sit on the yellow tiles of the kitchen windowsill with margarine between my toes, which is supposed to remove the tar. It is entirely unsuccessful and for the rest of the day I am beside myself with grief about missing this most treasured visit to my mother. There are times when I am not sure if she is still alive and my fear is that I will never see her again.

It must have been at this time that I write a sad little note to my mother in hospital:

'Dear Mummy, I hope you will get better soon and never get ill egen. We are going to hav a luvl time thes evening with presens. Goodbiy for kow my dear mummy. Love from diana to mummy giving her much love.

This rare visit might be around the time of her birthday, on June 9th. My brother John is allowed to visit her; as he arrives in the ward, he says, in a voice loud enough for everyone to hear, 'I always think that when a person reaches 40, they are *really* old.' No doubt my mother, who had had such a narrow escape from death, was feeling much older than her years. As my mother's birthday was only four days away from mine, on June 5th, there is also the added grief of having had my sixth birthday without my mother's warm presence and with little or no celebration. As I weep on that long afternoon I feel a sense of being beyond comfort…an inconsolable grief that cannot be contained. Perhaps in that weeping I am also expressing the anxiety of those long months of her absence when no one knows whether she will ever come home again.

When, eventually, my mother comes home to us, the only help we have in both house and garden is our live-in lady gardener, Miss Mack. There is also, for a time, a single mother with a little girl who comes to help us during my mother's convalescence.

But it soon becomes clear that it is my father who is now desperately ill. He has been feeling increasingly tired and unwell and has had difficulty in speaking, which is of course an essential aspect of his work! A combination of my mother's illness, the bombing that can be heard every night - with shrapnel sometimes hitting the house - the burden of a practice that has grown as younger analysts have been called up, and the responsibility of three children, has left him exhausted.

In a letter to his mentor C.G Jung, my father gives a description of the nightly bombing raids that surrounded our house:

The boys are just coming in with toy-carts full of bomb splinters and chunks of metal casing. We had a streak of bombs straddle the house last night; one fell among the trees just beyond the ditch at the bottom of the field and one in the wood the other side of the road. But the only damage was a couple of window casements blown out by the blast in the summer-house and some glass in the green house. That was at 8.30 in the evening. So now we all sleep down in the hall. Christopher is the only one of the children who shows signs of nervousness, although of course they all awoke with the blast with beating hearts and cried a bit. They were all asleep again very soon each holding the hand of a guardian angel.

It soon becomes necessary for my father to be treated in hospital. My brothers and I are to be sent away so that my mother can be with him in hospital. I am reluctant to leave. Perhaps there is some premonition; a child's ability to know what is afoot without a word being spoken. I cry; in fact, I am inconsolable. My father, sitting on the bed in our guest bedroom, comforts me. He takes me in his arms and cradles me, as one would a tiny child. He can no longer speak easily but I am comforted and feel held in a way that makes me know that I am secure in his love for me. This seems to be enough. We leave soon after this and I never see him again.

A stay in St. Thomas' Hospital confirms the diagnosis of an inoperable brain tumour. My father's physician, Dr. Evan Jones, tells us that he has only a few weeks to live. My brothers and I stay in Camberley with my godmother, our dear Midiboo (Evie D'Oyly), whose daughter would soon marry the young and still unknown, Laurens van der Post. It is a sedate and elderly household; one which is entirely unused to the pranks of three lively children. We are well looked after but soon become bored and homesick.

The house, Hocknorton Lodge, is situated right on the busy London Road. My brothers think that if we walk far enough along the road it will eventually bring us home to West Byfleet. They collect a small bundle of food and we set off one hot August morning. Mickey tells me we are just going out to pick blackberries. We walk until I am exhausted and then my brothers take it in turns to carry me. We pass a bread van and somehow manage to pay for a loaf; the dry bread is devoured between us. We walk for six miles before the police find us and take us back, ashamed and disappointed, to my godmother's house. As a punishment Mickey is made to scrub the tiled floor of the conservatory but we surreptitiously give him a helping hand. One can only imagine my godmother's distress and anxiety when she discovers her three charges have vanished. After this we are kept under very close surveillance.

Soon after this event, I am lying in bed one night but am not yet asleep. My godmother comes into my room, called 'The Blue Room'. She sits beside me on the bed and holds my hand. She tells me, very gently, that my father has now moved on; that he has been in St Thomas' Hospital in London, being looked after by nurses, but that he has now left hospital and has moved to a place called 'Heaven' where in future he will be looked after by angels. This seems fine to me. I accept this new situation expecting that one day he will be back again. For years, some part of me continued to expect him to return. My brothers, being older, have a greater understanding of the finality of death. I don't weep, nor do I mourn for my father. We don't attend the funeral, so the sense of finality that comes when the coffin is lowered into the ground is an experience we miss.

The news of my father's death reached Jung and his wife Emma. Emma wrote to my mother as soon as she was able - a letter dated September 21st 1943. The writing paper is edged with black; on the envelope is written in large black letters, 'Opened by the Examiners': the letter had been opened by the censors.

Emma writes:

My dear Anne,
   Like a terrible blow it came to us, this saddest of news of Peter's passing away. I hardly can believe it. We had heard only a couple of days before that he was ill, but didn't understand it was

such a dangerous thing, and now this! Poor Anne, I can't tell you how sorry I am for you, knowing what a terrific loss it means for you. I would like to be near you, so that I might show you my sympathy and maybe help you in some way or other, but as it is I can only hope that you may feel all I should like to express to you across the distance and that it may comfort you; be it ever so little.

Peter's last letter a few months (or weeks) ago seemed so positive and full of life, that I cannot understand how it is possible that he should leave us so soon. All the lovely memories connected with him and you come back to my mind; he was a very dear and true friend indeed and has helped me often just through his way and with his great kindness and understanding, so that in my heart he will always be alive.

If ever you feel that you can do it, I should appreciate enormously, if you could write me about him, how it came about and about the last time of his life, and also of you, my dear Anne and the children.

Our last visit with you is such a beautiful memory; you have been so lovely and so hospitable and I so hoped to see you again in not too far a future; now we can only be grateful for the beautiful things of the past and bend ourselves to the decision of Fate, although being unable to understand. I hope that you will be given the necessary strength and courage to accept it and face life again afterwards.

With my best love, Yours as ever, Emma Jung

My mother wrote to Emma Jung on 4th February 1944 in reply to Emma's letter of condolence. She thanks Emma for her ...

'... warm and dear letter. I was glad indeed to hear from you and hope my letter reached you, which I wrote while Peter was ill at St Thomas's Hospital.

I was with him the whole time, and I think he was deeply content and at peace; it seemed as if he knew the way and was ready to go. Death came with perfect gentleness and because he accepted death completely, I have been able to.

But it has been difficult learning to do without him – and I have longed to talk to you.

The children have been the most wonderful help – they are so dear and lovely. And Christopher is now launched on his war-time career, as a radio-mechanic in the Navy.

It was a very difficult year for us. Peter had been feeling more and more ill and sometimes bewildered – but no one knew what was wrong. It was only his extraordinary strength and courage which made it possible for him to keep going and to see all his patients up till the 6th August – for he was already finding it difficult to talk – and two weeks later he could not speak at all and his right side was paralysed.

I am so terribly sad that Peter was not able to finish his last book which he was so looking forward to, and had only just begun. But I am hoping that it will be possible to publish the first three chapters which he had finished, together with some of his collected papers.

Dear Emma – how long ago that Easter morning seems, when we climbed the hill at Camelot. That was a lovely holiday – and my heart is always glad when I think of it! And when I think of Peter.

With all my love to you and to C.G.

From Anne

Missing my father became a pain that has never really diminished. Perhaps this was neither recognized nor considered. That must also have been true for my brothers. John was sent to his boarding school at the age of nine, just a few days after our father's death. The sense of abandonment he experienced and his unhappiness at that school are things from which he has never entirely recovered. These wounds from the past affect everything we are and everything we do, and I am perfectly sure they influence the decisions we make in life.

Was it just a coincidence that I went to St. Thomas' to train as a nurse when I left school? Just chance that one of the patients referred to all St. Thomas' nurses as 'angels'? Was I still seeking the father I had never completely said goodbye to? Perhaps I thought that if only I could be one of his 'angel' nurses, I might find him again? In a sense I did find some quality of my father that I had been unconsciously seeking all my life. I went on to marry a Thomas' surgeon, a very fatherly man, whose own father, Alan Crockford, was a true, generous and loving father to me. So, in a strange way, I did perhaps discover some quality of my father there.

There are so many things to recall. My childhood returns to me now in a patchwork of laughter and tears, joys and sorrows, good days and bad. I can pick strands here and there and try to piece them all together. The war years permeated all the events of my childhood. I was just two when war broke out. There were days of unbroken sunshine and joyous times when my father was still with us and our family was together. His presence in our childhood was vitally important to us despite its brevity. I particularly remember bed times in my yellow cot; I wouldn't go to sleep until he had come to say good night and sing to me. His lullaby was to the tune of Brahm's song, *The Sandman,* but to words my father had invented. It went:

> He came from the land of Storey,
> Out of the East He came.
> He came with love and glory,
> And no one knew his name.
> He came with song and laughter
> To praise the happy hour.
> Tra,la.la.
> Tra la la la la la la
> La la la la la.

Another song was *The Tree in the Wood*, which gathered speed as he repeated each part of the tree in the refrain, 'The bird was in the nest, the nest was on the twig, the twig was on the branch, the branch was on the limb and the limb was on the tree.ee.ee; and the green grass grew around, around,

around, and the green grass grew around'. I hear his voice now as I remember the words!

My father died in 1943, when I was six and my brothers were nine and eleven. Then the clouds descended. Home had once felt like a secure place; now nothing was certain. The war was at its height, bombs were still dropping around us and my mother was frail after having spent six months or more in hospital. She had no immediate source of income and there were times when she wasn't sure how we would survive. This was not something of which we were consciously aware, but I imbibed it from my mother's sadness and endless worry.

Her worry seemed to be mostly about my brothers: how she would cope in bringing them up alone and how she could afford to educate them. The state schools at the time were simply not an option. Our situation, in wartime, was certainly not unusual. Many families were without a breadwinner. Most children of my age did not have a father at home because the majority of fathers were away fighting in the war. At 57, my father had been too old to take an active part in the war. It is possible we accepted our situation more readily because there were so many others in the same boat.

I remember it as a time when the sun no longer shone and my mother seldom smiled. She was easily reduced to tears by a chance remark, which I found very embarrassing. For the first time I was aware of her as someone who needed to be looked after; someone who needed my love and concern in order to survive. But also, of course, so that we all could survive! Children, like all little animals, have their own survival as their main concern. Without a mother, what would have become of us? My mother's survival became my main concern and the central theme of my life. I now realize that to a large extent it shaped me into the person I am today.

The luxury of the pre-war years had long vanished. There was no longer any help in the house, and only occasional help in the large four and a half acre garden. This was in stark contrast to the pre and early war years, when my parents employed a live-in maid, a cook, a resident nanny and a governess. There had also been two full-time gardeners who had looked after the large vegetable and fruit garden, the rose garden, herbaceous border and the lovely woodland area with azaleas and rhododendrons. They had also tended to the more exotic plants, which they carefully nurtured in the heated greenhouse. My father had also been a passionate gardener.

I have been thinking about my life and about the tears that haven't been shed and how these unshed tears can cast a long, long shadow in life. I had so little understanding at the time of the forever-ness of death and of the impact that my father's death would have on our lives. Children accept what happens to them in a matter of fact way and I don't remember recognizing my own sadness, or of considering the difficulties we experienced at home as a result of my father's death.

Chapter 3

School

*And then the whining schoolboy, with his satchel, and shining
morning face, creeping like a snail unwillingly to school.*
(Shakespeare: *As You Like It,* 1.iv)

I started school when I was four and have a clear memory of
my first day at Miss West's infant school. It may have been
my father who took me there in his Studebaker; being a
doctor, he was still able to obtain petrol during the war
years, although my mother's little Ford remained unused in
the garage until the war ended.

It was a tiny school with just three classrooms; a low,
single story building set in a large, suburban Surrey garden.
The children ranged in age from four to eight years old. The
main entrance at the front of the building led straight into
the classroom for the youngest children. The large 1920s
red brick house that was home to the Head teacher, Miss
West, stood across the wide lawn where our sports' days
were held.

I loved this school from the very first moment. I was
greeted by Miss West and passed into the care of one of the
older girls who 'shepherded' me during my first day. I don't
remember being shy, but I was almost immediately aware of
the far greater possibilities that school offered, compared
with the limited scope of an uninterested governess in the
nursery at home. My brothers had started school long before
and travelled by train every morning to a school called
Wallop, in Weybridge. My father would drive them to the
station and sometimes, on the days when he was working in
his consulting room in Mansfield Street, he accompanied
them on the train. He worked in London as a Jungian

analyst for three days a week and practised at home on the other days.

I longed to take part in 'proper' lessons but, above all, I longed for the companionship of other children, especially the chance to have a girl of my own age as a playmate. Boys were all very well but the games I enjoyed most were imaginative games; playing doctors and nurses, schools or mothers and fathers. Boys' games seemed for the most part to be contests of strength, prowess on bikes and ball games or playing with the Hornby electric train set in the loft. Here I was able to witness the wonders of the train track but never allowed to take part, except to arrange my farm animals in the fields beside the track. I could join in their games but could never compete with brothers who were five and three years older than me. I tried hard to develop my biceps by doing push-ups, and pull-ups on the rafters in the loft. I became adept at stunt riding on my boys' bicycle. This meant sitting on the handle bars facing backwards, riding the bike up the steep bank beside the oak tree on the big lawn, then sailing down the other side, without falling off. I made a good tomboy.

At school, I at last meet girls of my own age who enjoy playing the games I long to play. They even listen to what I say and sometimes even find me funny; a new experience altogether! Brothers can be helpful and even, in times of trouble, protective. But one thing that is a prevailing theme throughout my early life with my brothers is that I am definitely inferior in everything we do. I experience myself as the 'little sister' who can be tolerated but who, inevitably, is treated with a kind of dismissive affection.

At school I find, to my enormous surprise, that I am *somebody* and that among my contemporaries, I am in demand. I have two girlfriends, Jill Scott and Rosemary Oliver. They become frequent visitors to my house and I to theirs.

As Jill Scott lives in a large house just at the end of our tree-lined avenue, I am soon allowed to go there alone on my bike and play with her whenever I wish. She is an only child and is as starved of a playmate as I am. She has an amazing number of toys for a wartime child. I comment on the wonders of her nursery to my mother, who replies, 'Sometimes parents give too many toys to a child, instead of giving love,' which satisfies me, and I am never again envious of her wealth of lovely things. She is not a happy child and tells me of the cries she hears from her mother in the night when her parents are in bed. It makes me wonder, even at that early age, what goes on between a man and a woman in bed at night.

Rosemary Oliver has a rather prim mother but a truly lovely Daddy. He sometimes disappears under the table at teatime to eat his bread and jam, pretending to be a dog, and we find this uproariously funny. His wife, however, sits at the head of the table, stiff with disapproval, which makes it seem even funnier. I had never known grown-ups to be naughty!

I have a third friend at my infant school, a tall, gentle and rather pale boy of my own age called John Parry. He is not a rough and tumble boyish boy like my brothers but actually prefers to play with the girls. I think this is wonderful. I have never before met a boy who actually *enjoys* playing with girls, so he and I spend a lot of time together. When I am five or six he asks me to marry him. I accept at once. He doesn't want my best friend, Jill, to be left out, so he invites her to become his sister. Everyone is happy.

I find the lessons easy and excel at reading; I know my letters and can already read a little before beginning school. I have a book at home called *The Little Red Hen,* which I am able to read in its entirety. It may have been our governess who taught me to read. I enjoy maths and music and can sing beautifully. I play the part of a gypsy in a school performance and am asked to sing a solo called 'The

Wraggle Taggle Gypsies-o.' But at school if a child is slow to learn he or she fares badly. There is a small boy in my class who has trouble reading aloud. He is often made to stand in the corner wearing a dunce's cap. How cruel teachers could be!

I have a similar experience when I am older. At the age of eight we are already doing long division sums which are totally beyond me. The more our head teacher tries to explain it to me, the more baffled I become. Her insistence that I understand makes it increasingly impossible for me to take in what she is trying to tell me. She sees me as obstinate and assumes that I am deliberately refusing to understand. As a punishment I am banished to her large house across the lawn and made to sit at her dining room table, studying the sum until it is solved. I am unable to work it out; soon it is time to go home. I have been rather poor at maths ever since.

It isn't unusual for lessons to be interrupted by an air-raid warning, when we are all told to lie flat on the floor. These interruptions are rather exciting; seeing a doodlebug pass overhead is a thrilling experience. We seem to have no sense of danger or fear.

I become head girl at the age of eight and feel I have gained a certain respect and authority, which is impossible at home! I am a happy and self-confident child at this stage, even though my father had died two years previously and things are difficult at home. My enjoyment of school, however, is in no way affected.

We do not own a car after my father's death. My mother's small Ford remains in the garage but there is no longer any petrol available for civilian households. (In fact, my mother didn't ever obtain a driving licence after they were first introduced in 1945, and never again drove a car). The school is four miles from our house so my mother cycles there with me on the back of her bike. As I grow older and heavier she puts me on a bus at the top of

Sheerwater Road, just beside the Marris Convent School, and I manage the remaining three miles alone on the bus. By this time, both my brothers are away at boarding school.

One sunny afternoon I find myself walking in crocodile formation along the road leading from the school. Where we are going I don't remember; perhaps we are simply going for a walk, keeping strictly to the pavement, holding hands, two by two, our teacher walking at the front of the line. We are sometimes taken on nature walks to gather wild flowers, leaves, insects, fungi and wild fruits, which we study when we return to our classrooms.

I am holding the hand of my partner, a small boy. Suddenly, and without warning, he bites one of my fingers. It isn't so much the physical pain that affects me as the shock and the bruised feelings. I know, from my brothers, that it is 'sissy' to cry, so with monumental effort I hold in the tears but don't manage it entirely. A noise, something between a groan and a shout, comes from somewhere deep within me. The teacher wonders what on earth has happened. As I am frightened of letting the tears flow, I am unable to tell her. It feels so essential to hold on to feelings, for fear of being ridiculed.

Sports' days on the big lawn are very special occasions. It is important to me that my mother attends and I feel the need to win for her. I have been trained well by my brothers and can run faster than many girls and boys of my age. I am also, by the age of eight, the best in the school at high jump.

I am supple and well co-ordinated and spend much of my time at home walking on my hands, doing backbends and walking upside down like a crab. I can do successions of cartwheels until I fall over completely dizzy and laugh in the grass while the sky spins above me. I feel at ease in my body and can trust it to do what I want.

In my early life I must have transferred my need for a strong father figure on to Mickey, who was a support to me and, when he was at home, a lovely companion. My mother recorded the following dream of mine on 8th December 1945, which shows how important he had become to me:

The two shepherds were on one hill in the garden at Reed House and about four wise men were on the other hill and Jesus was lying between them. The oldest shepherd (who was Mickey), said to the younger one (who was me): 'Don't take any notice what the audience say about not eating grass; it's good for you to eat grass; all the other shepherds do'. And I agreed. And the wise men copied us. So, we went on eating grass and Jesus did too and he ate a brown leaf. Then suddenly he died and we all sang over him. The audience had vanished. We were really half sheep and half shepherds. The end.

I become too old for Miss West's school, so my mother sends me to a junior school some distance from home. My first day at the new school is traumatic. My mother takes me to the bus on the pillion of her bike. I have to change buses in Woking and catch one going to Chobham. The PNEU (Parents' National Education Union) school, called Flexlands, is near the village bus stop. I am full of anticipation at the thought of being in this 'big' school that my two brothers had attended before me, and it feels like an important stage in growing up. I expect to love it and to be liked by everyone, just as I had been at Miss West's.

I arrive alone at the school and am shown into my classroom of eight year olds. My arrival is greeted with total silence as the whole class eyes me up and down. No one comes forward to welcome me. Finally, Pat Straker, the queen bee of this unwelcoming class, addresses me with the unexpected comment, 'pull down your knickers'. I blush deep red as everyone titters. All my anticipation and eagerness melt away and I long to return home. That first day is the longest of my life. It is a very dejected little girl that my mother meets from the bus that afternoon. She knows at once that something is amiss, but it is some time before I am able to speak about what had happened.

The school improves a little after I make a friend, Patsy Beard, who is also the butt of Pat Straker's catty tongue. We play together at break time and stand by one another when the going gets tough. It is my first experience of real nastiness and teaches me the all-important lesson that life is not always kind and that being disliked is part and parcel of living. In my very sheltered life it had never occurred to me that people were not always loving and kind, even though I was well aware of the normal rough and tumble of sibling rivalries and I had plenty of experience of a brother who was not always gentle! But somehow that was different; I was aware that deep down, despite the teasing and fighting, we *did* love each other. I learned to be cautious in relation to my peers at Flexlands and I think became a much less outgoing and confident child as a result. My mother recognized my unhappiness and after only two terms she sent me to another school.

Diana and Mother

My mother was depressed for many years after my father's death. I was more affected by this than my brothers because I was alone with her at home. It was not always a good place to be. I think I must have felt that life was very precarious and that home was not a particularly safe place. A dream I had in October 1944 gives a strong sense of my basic insecurity.

Well, I was on the balcony and I went back to the study (which was where the bathroom is now) and then I went back on the balcony again and went along the edge of the balcony towards the study, but there were no railings to hold on to and I fell down and was killed.

My mother's depression affected me and I became withdrawn and lacking in confidence, which in turn impacted on my ability to learn at school. Aware of this, my mother sent me to weekly board with a family called Maxwell Eve when I was nine, so that I could attend an unusually liberal and imaginative school called Hurtwood, in Peaslake, Surrey.

The headmistress of Hurtwood, Miss Jewson, had a particular gift with children and her teaching ideas were most unusual for the time. She created a giant monopoly board for our history lessons, around which the whole class gathered. It began with William the Conqueror and ended with WWII, which in 1947 had been over for little more than a year. You can imagine how much we enjoyed these lessons! She made learning seem like a wonderful game, which, perhaps, is how it *should* be.

On a sunny summer's day she would sometimes stop all lessons and allow the whole school to spend the rest of the day in the swimming pool. During the freezing winter of 1947, when the entire country was in the grip of a harsh frost from January until March, my friend Jancis and I would walk to school through a frozen world of snow and ice. I remember how every single holly leaf had a perfect replica in ice attached to it. Miss Jewson was a fine artist and sculptor. When the snow first fell she sculpted, for our delight, animals that were as unfamiliar with snow as one could imagine: a crocodile, elephant, rhinoceros and a splendid giraffe. The biggest of all was an enormous whale. Although they were not life-size, they were certainly realistic and they remained with us, as part of our playground, all winter.

As well as being the head teacher, Miss Jewson also acted as a magistrate, or possibly a JP (justice of the peace). She was familiar with legal proceedings and felt it was important for us to learn about the law. One day I am having my violin lesson in the dining room with Mereddy, (I think her real name must have been Miss Ready). I am surprised by the cook, who rushes out of the kitchen brandishing a carving knife. She pretends to slit my throat then pushes me under the piano and informs me that I am dead. The alarm is raised that a murder has taken place and school comes to a standstill.

For two whole days we sit in court. As I am the only pupil who knows who the murderer is I have to stay silent, although I am on the jury. Miss Jewson is, of course, the judge, and others play the parts of witnesses, jurors, relatives, and members of the public. There are even journalists, who write up the entire event for the school journal. The court proceedings are conducted in an entirely realistic way; the cook is eventually apprehended and convicted of murder. Although we know it is not for real, none of us will ever forget how a court procedure is conducted.

Miss Jewson, known to all of us as Duta, encourages our imaginative and creative play. During break times we create a village out of bracken in the neighbouring wood. Each of us has our own house, and there are also shops, a bank, a well-stocked pub, a police station, church, hotel and even a prison. There is also a builder who can construct a house for children who are too small to build their own. A boy called Dan Wickstead, who is my senior by a year, falls in love with me and asks me to marry him. We are duly married in the bracken church and he presents me with a ring. For a time we do everything together and (I think) even 'move in together', sharing a larger bracken house during playtimes. I remember the song I often sing to him which is, in my child's way, attached to ardent feelings for Dan. It goes:

> Little John, Bottle John lived on a hill
> And a blithe little man was he;
> He won the heart of a little mermaid
> Who lived in the deep blue sea:
> And on every evening she used to sit
> And sing on the rocks by the sea:
> 'Oh Little John, Bottle John,
> Pretty John, Bottle John,
> Won't you come out to me?

The passion fades after a time. He insists on calling out, ''ello darlin' every time we pass each other in school and I begin to find this too embarrassing, so we go through a formal divorce. Afterwards, he chases me during break times. Amazingly, I can run faster than him and am very seldom caught.

During the week I stay with the Maxwell Eve family whose daughter, Jancis, is my age and is in the same class. My mother collects me from the bus in Guildford every Friday and returns me on a Sunday evening. During the long, cold spell it is impossible for me to go home so I remain with the Maxwell Eves for several weeks. At times I am very homesick. A painting that hangs on the wall by my bed represents my longing for home: it is of a brown-furrowed field, a man ploughing and an occasional wintry tree.

Although Jancis and I do not become close friends and our friendship doesn't continue after I leave Hurtwood (even though we later go to the same public school), we do have lovely times together. I am happy with the Maxwell

Eve family, in spite of my occasional homesickness, and they are kind to me. Jancis and I are both learning to play the violin and we like to practice together. Sometimes we put on a classical record and while one of us is the conductor, waving a baton in time to the music, the other pretends to be the entire orchestra.

While staying with this family, I experience something of marital strife for the first time. Mr Maxwell Eve is a difficult man and his wife is large and rather formidable. Jancis and her older brother (who is only at home during his school holidays) seem to be in awe of both their parents. There is no misbehaving or answering back. Jancis speaks in such a tiny voice it is often difficult to hear her. (It is interesting that she was later to become a speech therapist!). Both children seem to be terrified of their father. I don't know if he ever struck either of them, but he frequently shouts, particularly at his wife, if something upsets him. At the top of his voice he shouts, 'Wait a minute!' and 'Be quiet!' And everyone is, sometimes for the duration of a meal. As I am the only one who is not afraid of him, I chatter on regardless. He is always kind to me, but I did wonder whether abusive things had ever occurred in relation to his children as they remained in such abject terror of him. I remember remarking to my mother, who at home tended to wait on us all hand and foot, 'It's different in the Maxwell Eve household; there, it's the children who are the slaves.' What amazed me most of all was that the children simply never complained or refused to do anything. Jancis remained a frightened little mouse at our senior school and never really escaped, inwardly, from her father's terrifying presence.

The rigidity and formality of life at home with the Maxwell Eves is in stark contrast to the freedom of school; I have never been as happy at a school before. Unfortunately, my time there comes to a sudden end. Duta, with her great heart, too often waives the fees for those who cannot afford to pay. As a result, the school is declared bankrupt and forced to close.

I return home to attend a local school called Langsmead that could hardly be more of a contrast to Hurtwood. Two unmarried sisters run it and apply the old-fashioned method of learning by rote. The teaching is pedestrian and as lacking in imagination as Duta's teaching was creative. However, I am happy to be back at home and, best of all, my closest friend Nicola Grierson, who attended Hurtwood as a boarder, comes to live with us, as her father has been posted to Germany.

We cycle the 4 miles to school together and sit next to each other during lessons. We are so close that we don't make any other friends. I remain at Langsmead School for about two years, from the age of ten to twelve. It is blissful to have a girl companion at home and to be able to enjoy games that are impossible to play with brothers. We each have a doll; Nicola's is Rosemary and mine is Anthony. (I still have him; when I look at him I remember the real joy I felt in caring for this first 'baby'!) To our minds these are not just dolls, they are our children. Every morning before school we wash and dress them, give them their bottles of milk and put them in their prams in the garden. As soon as we are home in the afternoon we bring them in, play with them, feed them and then tuck them up in their cots next to our beds.

I don't think Nicola and I ever quarrel but my mother's overt admiration of her physical beauty and her veiled comments about my untidiness, possibly make me a little jealous of her. Nicola is exceptionally lovely and becomes the most beautiful and sophisticated young woman. Both my brothers were later to love her, but it was Mickey who she would become fond of. It is probably because our friendship was so important to me that I named my first daughter Nicola.

Every Saturday my mother takes us both for swimming

lessons at the YWCA (Young Women's Christian Association) pool in Tottenham Court Road. An Olympic coach called Mrs Hughes gives us lessons, and I develop a great ambition to become an Olympic swimmer. On the way home we spend our pocket money on delicious food for our Saturday midnight feasts. We call these Saturday trysts our 'Orgyanimous', in order to keep them secret from my mother. But of course she knows and sometimes contributes an extra delicious treat to our feast. Food is still rationed so what we eat would seem rather unappetizing today. The pièce de résistance is a tin of sweetened condensed milk, which we suck through a small hole in the top of the tin. We also have chocolate powder and nuts and raisins. It all seems utterly delicious to us.

During the summer I develop a temperature, which persists for weeks. I am confined to a bed in my mother's study. Nicola is also unwell for a time and we spend lovely days, playing together. As the doctor can find nothing wrong, I am sent to St Peter's hospital in Chertsey, where I receive a diagnosis of pyrexia of unknown origin. I have various tests and watch, fascinated, as the nurses scurry to and fro in their pretty uniforms. It is an adult ward - apart from one other child - and the women of every shape, size and social class are kind and attentive to me. I decide that I would one day like to become a nurse; perhaps it is the pretty uniforms that convince me! Every evening my mother makes the journey by bus – a two-hour round-trip at least – to visit me; I am quite oblivious to the difficulties of ferrying me hither and thither without a car. Her devotion is incredible.

The week in hospital works wonders and my temperature never returns. However, I think my mother is aware that her depression is having a debilitating effect on me. I am sent away for the rest of the term to stay with the Fawcett family in Ickleton, near Saffron Walden, and for a few weeks I become a pupil at the small house school that their daughter, Teresa, attends. What becomes of Nicola is not clear but her parents may have returned home by this time. The visit to the Fawcett family proves to be a good time for me. I feel immediately at home and as though I belong in this warm and generous family.

Chapter 4

Cambridge

The stacks, like blunt impassive temples, rise
Across flat fields against autumnal skies.
The hairy-footed horses plough the land,
Or as in prayer and meditation stand
Upholding square, primeval, dung-stained carts,
With an unending patience in their hearts.

(Cambridge: by Frances Cornford)

My mother was often advised about the need to move from her big nine bedroom Surrey house with its large garden. Maintaining it was a struggle, although letting half of it also provided her with an income and companionship for us both. She thought it would be a good idea to move to Cambridge, as Mickey would be going up to Cambridge University to read medicine the following year. With this plan in mind, she took me for an interview at the Cambridgeshire County School for Girls. I sat a brief exam in headmistress Miss Battensby's study and was put into class 2A, the year's top academic stream.

I started at the school the following September. This was also the beginning of the time I spent with the Cornford family and a very different way of life. The experience of living with such an unusual, bohemian and intellectual family was to have a profound effect on my development and on my future interests.

The Cornford family connection stemmed from the friendship that developed between my father, Frances Cornford and her husband, the Plato scholar Francis Cornford, at the beginning of the 20th century. My father was a medical student at Cambridge University and he became attached to a left-wing circle of intellectuals which included the writers, artists and poets who surrounded Rupert Brook.

Frances used to speak to me about my youthful father; a tall, handsome rowing blue, who was gifted in every way and universally loved by both men and women. His energy and extraversion were legendary; according to Frances, when he entered a room he had the effect of a mighty gust of wind. Everyone would instantly be aware of his presence. For Frances, who was profoundly introverted, this could be overwhelming.

I am twelve years old when I go to live with the Cornford family and I am the only child (apart from a two-year-old boy called Daniel) among a group of young adults. It is the autumn of 1949 and just four years since the war ended. There was no school near our Surrey home that my mother felt would give me the kind of education in which she believed. At that time boarding school was not an option; my brothers' school fees were already stretching my mother's meagre income to the limit.

I remember one particular evening. We are sitting at table for the evening meal. The Estonian cook, Helga, has cooked a cheap dish, which we have every week: spaghetti with a tomato and onion sauce, with cheese sprinkled on top. No one is paying much attention to the food. Frances Cornford, a poet and grandchild of Sir Charles Darwin, sits at the head of the table. She is talking to the guest on her right who is her cousin, the artist Robin Darwin. Frances has gentle, deep-set eyes and a prominent forehead. Her dark hair is in a net and she is dressed in a flowing brown skirt with a wrap around her shoulders. She speaks with a passionate intensity. All the young are listening and interjecting in the conversation.

Opposite me are two young couples: Frances's son Hugh, a newly qualified doctor, and his wife Jean. Beside

Hugh is his younger sister, Clare and her husband, Cecil Chapman. To my right is a young man called Horace Barlow who is still a student at Cambridge and is also a distant cousin of Frances. Horace is young enough to be a companion for me. I ask him to tell me about his studies, but all I remember is the fact that he was going through some kind of philosophical life experience. I think this was also a form of rebellion against any kind of conformity, which included giving up washing. As I was sitting next to him I was well aware of this! I asked him what his problem with washing was all about. He replied that if one washes it is an admission that one is dirty. It seemed to be preferable to stay unwashed rather than admit to being unclean. The Cornford family seemed to accept this shaggy, unwashed individual just as he was, and I too learned to grow fond of him.

On my other side is Frances's grandson, James Cornford, who has lived at Conduit Head with Frances since his childhood. Now seventeen, James is in the sixth form at Winchester College and is well able to hold his own in the adult conversation around the table. I enjoy it when he is there as it means there is someone closer to my age to whom I can talk, and who treats me with a certain deference, unlike my two brothers. Frances adopted James after her son John, who was James' father, was killed in the Spanish Civil War. John was a Cambridge graduate, a published poet and a brilliant young man who died in his early twenties for the cause in which he passionately believed. He despised his parent's bourgeois values and lived his communist beliefs with all the passion of youth. After graduating from Cambridge, he lived in London with the daughter of a lorry driver who became pregnant before he left for Spain. She later married and had a large family but was happy to allow her first born, James, to be brought up by his grandmother. James was a gentle boy with a thick crop of dark hair and a mature manner that far exceeded his years. He had grown accustomed throughout his life to the daily play of words and ideas around the dinner table; a diet of intellectual banter that was very much more exciting than the food. No one seemed to either care or to notice what was eaten!

On this particular evening, I am hungry after a long day at school and an early start in my small attic room, in order to practice my violin, before catching the bus to school. The food has been served and Frances leads the conversation, which is an appraisal of contemporary poets. Stephen Spender and Walter de la Mare are discussed; both are close friends of Frances. A lively discussion then follows with regard to Dame Edith and Osbert Sitwell. I have never heard of them and don't even know what they do. There is a difference of opinion as to whether they are the leading lights of modern literature and poetry or whether they are too self-absorbed and pretentious to warrant a place among the elect. My mind wanders, as it often does. I don't much care either way. I am just wondering whether my mother will allow me to keep a guinea pig, when Frances turns to me and says, 'What do you think Dinny? Do you think the Sitwells are among the Greats in present day literature?' I have no idea what my reply was, but I remember that I am rather flattered that she should look to me for an opinion. I don't even know what I would say if I were asked that question today!

In Frances I found the most lovely companion; perhaps she took the place of the grandmother I had never had. When she was available, she was a grown-up who was entirely accessible to a child. I sometimes accompanied her when she gave readings of her poems to Cambridge audiences. She was very unassuming and read in a gentle, somewhat quavery voice; when, on one occasion she heard a recording of herself reading on the radio, she was horrified by what she deemed to be, 'my horribly affected voice'.

Every Sunday she went to the morning service at the Round Church in Cambridge. I don't think she could drive, so we travelled by taxi and she would drop me off at King's College Chapel, where I loved to listen to the wonderful choir. She once told me that her family was severely critical of her Christian faith, almost as though this was a sacrilege to her grandfather's memory. No member of the Darwin family would ever have dreamt of going to church. Frances said, 'We always used to go to church at Christmas. One day I simply discovered it was all true.' So, despite family criticism, she had attended church ever since.

Frances would talk to me with the same respect and seriousness as she would to an adult, asking my opinion on matters concerning her family, her friends, how she should lay the table for the evening meal and for how many; laying the table was a little evening ritual; her only domestic task. As the Cornfords kept open house, it was impossible to know beforehand how many would be eating with us.

Each day had an unvarying routine for Frances. She would have breakfast in bed, get up at 10.00 am and entertain any guests who happened to be staying. At 2.00 pm exactly, she would disappear to her little cabin in the garden to write. She put a handwritten notice on the door saying, 'Out 'til 4.00 pm'. This time was sacrosanct, and all the family knew it was not possible to disturb her during those hours.

I loved her passionately and longed one day to be able to be like her, to write like her and to treat all humanity with the same gentle reverence and respect. I never heard her say a critical word about anyone, although all the young people were the most appalling intellectual snobs. I remember that the royal family in particular came in for some fierce criticism.

I played with Daniel, Jean and Hugh's small boy, taking him for walks and telling him stories. He became so attached to me that when their second son, Stephen, was born, Jean and Hugh asked me to be his godmother. I believe on this occasion, they must have gone to church! I was delighted to accept, although at twelve I'm not sure how seriously I understood my godmotherly responsibilities. Stephen is now also living in the North of England, so we occasionally see one another.

Frances's close friends included some of the leading poets of the time. Stephen Spender and his wife, Natasha Latin, were frequent visitors. I remember Stephen as a kindly and unassuming man who was friendly and gentle with me, a shy young girl. His wife, Natasha, was exotic and very lovely. She had a busy career as a concert pianist, but I was never lucky enough to hear her play. Frances's cousin, the artist and writer, Gwen Raverat, would also spend much of her time at Conduit Head, although as she lived in Cambridge, she seldom spent the night.

Another close friend was Walter de la Mare. Frances would sometimes go to stay with him. I remember her telling me that de la Mare's daughter was such a gifted dressmaker she was able to cut out a dress without a pattern and could do this with the material spread out over her knee. I have never fathomed how this was possible! On one occasion, when Frances was going to visit de la Mare, I begged her to ask him to write a poem for me. I had a book of his poems for children, and knew one or two from memory;

> *Has anybody seen my Mopser,*
> *A comely dog is he*
> *With hair of the colour of a Charles the Fifth*
> *And teeth like ships at sea*
> *His tail it curls straight upwards,*
> *His ears stand two abreast*
> *And he answers to the simple name of Mopser*
> *When civilly addressed.*

And another comes to mind:

Jemima is my name
But oh, I have another
My father always calls me Meg
And so do Bob and mother.
Only my sister, jealous of
The strands of my bright hair,
Jemima, Mima Mima!
Calls mocking up the stair.

I was thrilled when she returned with the following poem, written in his beautiful hand writing, in my autograph book:

The cool clear flowers of early spring
In summer's ardours are forgot.
But two are here, transcending hers,
A primrose and a forget me not.

Within the pages of a book
Their coloured petals, paper dry
Though faint and frail, their secret keep
They fade but do not die.

Signed at the bottom, *Walter de la Mare, Christmas 1949*

What a treasure this was for a little girl, to have a poem especially written for her!

Frances also wrote a poem for me:

Frances Cornford can but think,
She may mar this perfect pink
With her pen's unworthiness,
Has she blotted? Heavens YES.

(Here she has smudged the ink)

Today I wonder in what ways I have been influenced by life with the Cornford family. Perhaps now that I have stopped working as a psychotherapist it may be possible to fulfil a lifelong ambition to write; even to write poetry. I now have the time to read poetry in the way I did when I was young, when it was a musical, auditory, almost sensual experience. So different from the more academic approach we were taught at school.

I remember the hum of after-dinner chat in the Cornford household, when conversation flowed from subject to subject - almost in a stream of consciousness way - as it moved from poetry to people to the wider family and the wider world. I remember relations such as the Darwins, the Wedgewoods and the Peseys were often referred to. The politics of the day and new ideas relating to science and astronomy were all grist to the mill. How different it all was from the daily banter, rivalry and ribaldry of our mealtime conversations at home!

In the evenings I sit mostly in silence, drinking in the adult talk but understanding only fragments, as one might when listening to a foreign language. I collect the stub ends of the cigarettes they all smoke, (there were no filters in those days) and stuff the tobacco into the butt of a small bubble pipe I have bought at Woolworths. I then puff away, pretending to be grown-up. In a sense, I am treated as a grown-up, in that no one ever reprimands me or reminds me to go to bed, get up, go to school or do my homework. I am made to feel entirely responsible for myself.

After a few terms of living with the Cornfords my mother feels that I need the company of others closer to my age, and once again approaches the Fawcett family, with whom I had spent such happy weeks two years previously. The Fawcett family lives in the village of Ickleton, which lies twelve miles to the south of Cambridge. Their daughter, Teresa, is two years younger than me. Her two older brothers are away at boarding school. Frances writes a letter after my mother has made the decision that I should leave the Cornford household.   The letter is dated 24th October, 1949. She writes:

'But all the same I hate the thought of not having her. Dear and tender Dinny, so alive and yet so delicately withdrawn, who never is an anxiety or trouble. And it makes me v. happy to think that tho' she certainly will want to go to the Fawcetts, she won't like the moment of leaving either, because she has settled in and become a part of us. Possibly she might be back in the summer?? But we mustn't think ahead that far.'

She writes again on November 21st in answer to my mother's letter:

'Thank you much for your letter. I am so grateful to hear this time has been fruitful for you, as well as lonely - even desolate - as it must have been without Dinny.
    Dear Anne, she really is a jewel. I've never known such a delicate independence of character. Both in-born and acquired. Everybody who comes to stay (this week-end the Salamans), say the same thing. This being so, that you've given me a spiritual gift with Dinny, would you be cross if just before Xmas, I returned your cheque?'

Teresa becomes for me the younger sister I had always longed for. We enjoy the same games of imagination; as we walk around their lovely garden on stilts, we pretend to be knights in combat: Sir Gawain and the Green Knight. When we climb the walnut tree at the bottom of the garden, we are tree people who create their own arboreal world. We play with our extensive Britain animal farms for days on end, remembering each day to feed the animals and milk the cows. Our days of imaginative play together are some of the happiest of my childhood.
    We wander the country lanes on our ponies, Cuckoo and Frolic. Mine was Frolic, who was borrowed from friends and had seen better days; he could scarcely trot, let alone

'frolic'. The River Cam borders the Fawcett's Mill House; in the summer we enjoy swimming, and diving into the Mill Pond from the wall that extends from the old mill. It is a child's paradise. On the banks of the river they have a gaily-painted gypsy caravan in which Teresa and I sometimes sleep and where I do my homework in the summer months.

It is a very different experience for me to be in a home with both a mother and a father. Anne is a lovely and creative mother who has been a Froebel teacher and can stimulate children's imaginations and create a perfectly enchanted setting. Robby is a gentle man; I have a special fondness for him and he, I believe, for me. Robby reads to Teresa and me by their fireside every evening: Wilkie Collins' *The Woman in White* and Charlotte Brontë's *Jane Eyre.* I can hear his voice now as I remember these books. Robby is learning the piano and practices diligently every day. He encourages me in my violin practice and likes to hear me sing.

At school I have an English teacher called Miss Turner, who also encourages my singing. She has an imaginative and stimulating method of teaching and is able to bring Shakespeare alive in a way that makes the action and poetry become meaningful and accessible. We are reading *As You Like It* in class and acting it at the same time. I am playing the part of Jacques and Miss Turner asks me to sing the song, 'Blow, blow thou winter wind'. I already know this song and am able to give a fair performance for the class. Miss Turner says, 'You have a beautiful voice and should become a professional singer.' These words were, perhaps, to have a bearing on my eventual career.

Perhaps it is as a result of Miss Turner's encouragement that I enter a singing competition in Cambridge. The song set for my age group is called *I've been roaming.* I learn it from memory and have one or two lessons with the wife of the then conductor of the King's College Choir Boys, Boris Ord (who was to make the choir world famous). His wife had been a professional singer; she was to be the first person who taught me how to breathe and how to sing a musical phrase. The song began:

I've been roaming,
I've been roaming
  Where the meadow dew is sweet,
  And I'm coming, and I'm coming
With its pearls upon my feet.

I stand on stage in front of a large audience, quite confident in my ability to please the judges. I don't win. The other girls in my class are accomplished performers of popular music and have all studied singing for some time. I am highly commended and encouraged enough to want to continue to sing.

Diana, Mickey, Anne and John, outside Reed House

Chapter 5

Holidays

If all the year were playing holidays, to sport would be as tedious as to work; but when they seldom come, they wished for come.
(Shakespeare: King Henry 1V, Part 1, 1.ii)

Since my father's death we had only taken three holidays as a complete family. Soon after his death we were given a holiday at Bryanston School, staying in the sanatorium. The situation beside the River Stour was lovely, with open countryside and exciting woodlands to explore.

But it was the holiday we were to spend on the Island of Mull which still glows in my memory. We take a sleeper from London and arrive in Oban early the following morning. To me, Scotland is a far away foreign land; this is the first time I have ventured beyond English shores. I look out of the window from my top bunk to see trees and fields, houses and streets that look all too familiar. I am somehow expecting the grass, flowers, trees and houses to have a distinctly foreign and unfamiliar appearance. I say to my mother, with a sense of let down and disappointment, 'I think Scotland is very like England in many ways.'

From Oban we take the MacBrayne ferry across to Mull. I stand on deck, the wind in my face, carried away by a sense of ecstasy and excitement, singing *Speed Bonny Boat* at the top of my voice. This feels to me like the ultimate adventure. At Craignure we catch a bus to the distant farm in Ardalanish, near Bunessan, where we are to spend the next three weeks. It is my first view of the mountains and of the craggy moorlands that give Mull its sense of unpeopled wilderness.

The farm stands alone in acres of wild meadows with the rocky, barren hillside rising behind. We are welcomed by the Campbell family, Mr and Mrs Campbell and their four grown up children, who are all still living at home. The farm is so remote that none of them have yet found anyone to marry. The eldest, Calem, is 27, then Mary Anne and Mary follow. The youngest son is Roddy, who is 21 but has a mental age similar to mine; I have just celebrated my 10th birthday. I love him dearly and spend much of the holiday in his company, helping him to milk the cows.

I soon develop the skill of hand-milking. One cow, Buttercup, happily allows her milk to flow for me. Roddy takes me for rides over the hills on the back of his carthorse; we gallop like the wind to a place high above the tree line, while I hold onto him for dear life. On one of these thrilling excursions Roddy asks me to marry him. I accept of course, though I'm not prepared to marry just yet! He tells me stories of his brave exploits; one was about a girlfriend who had fallen into the cup he had won for bravery. The silver cup was one mile high, the biggest the world had ever known. Roddy's girlfriend had climbed a tall ladder in order to admire the cup's glory from inside and had fallen headlong into its mighty interior. He had then climbed the ladder after her and lifted the mile high ladder inside the cup to bring her to safety. Of course, I believe every word of this story. He is for me the bravest of the brave.

For the three weeks of our stay in Mull the sun shines. Just a short walk from the farm is a beach with miles of white sand, rock pools and a total absence of people. The walk from the farm to the beach takes us down a grassy path along the cliff top with a view over the sea to Iona. There is a veritable garden of wild flowers along the way. I stop to gather them as we walk, counting at least 30 different species - more varieties than I have ever seen before. We seldom meet another person during our daily visits to the beach. We swim in the sea, explore the rock pools, collect cowry shells and semi-precious stones, make elaborate castles in the sand and run around gloriously naked.

It is an experience of paradise for us all. It is our first real holiday since the war and my father's death and it is as though life could once again be joyous and carefree. For my mother, also, it is a time of contentment and healing after so many stressful years. I remember her going with Mickey, then just 15, to a ceilidh in the local village hall and dancing with one of the local men. It is the first time I had recognized that my mother was an attractive woman and someone men would want to dance with.

The only shadow cast on this holiday for me was that it coincided with the wedding of our half-brother, Christopher. He was only 22 years old, but because of his inherited fortune (which had come to him on his 21st birthday, through his mother, Hilda Davidson, who had died when he was only two years old), it wasn't necessary for him to wait 'til he was earning a living.

Christopher had met a girl whilst serving in the Fleet Air Arm in Malta during the final year of the war. Visiting a café with a fellow sailor, he had seen a young woman behind the counter serving the men their drinks. Christopher was struck by her youth and beauty and commented to his companion, 'I am going to marry that girl.' And so it was, about two years later. Unfortunately, by the time Chris and Pat had arranged their wedding our holiday plans were already in place and it was impossible to change the dates. I loved Christopher and dearly wished to be present. It would have been the first wedding I had attended and it's possible that I might have been their bridesmaid. But it was not to be.

* * *

I remember one summer holiday in particular. I am twelve and Mickey, aged seventeen, is home from his public school, Bryanston. He suggests we take a camping holiday together. We set off on our bikes, carrying all our camping equipment, to where our wooden Canadian canoe is moored, close to a weir on the River Wey. We padlock our bikes and leave them in a shed, pack all the equipment into the canoe and set off down river.

We paddle well together. Mickey is an oarsman and is captain of rowing at school. He sits behind me, steering the canoe from the rear thwart and I sit on the floor of the canoe in the bow. He sits tall, his long brown legs splayed out, looking relaxed, focussed and at ease. We paddle to Weybridge, where we join the River Thames. The weather

Mickey

is lovely; a light breeze stirs the water and the sun shimmers on the ruffled surface, making us squint in the bright light. We are silent. We paddle in unison, lulled by the ripple and splash of the water as we dip our paddles and pull with strong, even strokes. We are running with the current, but the power of his strokes propels us with ease along the widening river. My strokes make little difference to our speed.

The sun begins to go down and our arms are aching. We find a place to pitch the tent on the river bank, beside a willow tree. I take my rod and cast, once, twice, three times. Then, to my amazement I find a fish on my little hook. We don't know what type it is, but we are soon grilling it on a fire. We have bread, cheese and salad with us, all of which makes a good meal, and all the more delicious for having made it ourselves. Our appetites are sharpened by exercise and a day in the open air. We laugh together and sing rounds by the campfire as darkness falls. It is cosy inside the tent in our sleeping bags and we are soon asleep. These are good, treasured memories.

My brother Mickey was care-ful...that is to say... full of care. He looked after his little sister and tried, as he grew older, to take a father's place. We did many activities together. He was clever with his hands and particularly loved carpentry and he taught me the joy of creating things from wood. We grew all the vegetables together in my mother's garden, when it was no longer possible to employ a gardener. We shared a record player which he had in his bedroom, with a speaker in my room, so we would go to sleep listening to Bach's Brandenburg Concertos, Nos 4 or 6; to Bach's Suite No. 3 and the lovely Air on a G string; to Mozart's Jupiter symphony or to Handel's Water Music. Our supply of LPs was limited!

Later, Mickey invited me to Cambridge. I was fêted by all his friends and invited to May Balls. I was a rented-out sister for the many young men who were still too shy to approach a young woman and ask her out.

After Cambridge he hoped to go to St. Thomas' Hospital to train as a doctor. His ambition was to become a plastic surgeon; to transform the lives of those who had become disfigured or injured, in the way that the famous plastic surgeon, Sir Archibald McIndoe at East Grinstead, had rebuilt the lives of fighter pilots who had suffered horrendous burns during WWII. But this was never fulfilled. He was killed in a motor accident when he was 24. My mother rang me one morning while I was preparing breakfast for the family for whom I was au pairing in Philadelphia.

At the time I remember feeling nothing. What can you feel when half of your world is suddenly blown away? I continued making the breakfast. That night in bed, I wept.

Being so far from home, I found it difficult to connect to the reality of what had happened. I was in a state of suspended grief. Everything around me felt strangely unreal, as though I was divorced from reality. I went home by boat. My mother was clear she didn't want me to fly; did flying represent too great a risk? It meant I arrived too late for the funeral. The next few weeks passed like a dream. Perhaps I didn't know how to mourn. Was it as it had been with the death of my father, similar to the childish belief I held that my father's death wasn't really forever?

Was I still looking for an older, caring man when I eventually married David? He too loved to sail, to make things out of wood and to camp and live in the open air. He too wanted to become (and eventually succeeded in becoming) a plastic surgeon. In David, was I looking for the father and the brother who had died? Both my father and brother were such an essential part of the stability and affirmation of my world. Perhaps it wasn't until David's death, when I was 44, that I was truly and profoundly able to mourn the loss of all three.

It was in my 12th year that Mickey introduced me to a sailing club on the Norfolk Broads where my brothers and I spent a week or two of every Easter and summer holidays until I left school. The Theta Club was run by Jack and Molly Pritchard. They had acquired an old landing barge, 'The Ark', near to Thurne Mouth, which was securely moored on the northern bank of the River Thurne. The Pritchards had a holiday house nearby in the village of Thurne.

The original members of the Theta Club were all from Bryanston School, which was the school that the Pritchard sons, Jonathan and Jeremy, attended. My brothers, also Bryanstonians, were among the first people to join the club. Other children were the offspring of artists and literary families, many of whom had flats in London's concrete building, known as The Lawn Road Flats in Belsize Park (which was also home to Jack and Molly). These flats had been created in the 1930s in the Bauhaus tradition by the architect, Wells Coates, as an experiment in collective living for left-wing intellectuals. They were inhabited almost entirely by artists and avant-garde families.

Other members of the Theta Club included William, the son of the cartoonist Osbert Lancaster and Judith, the daughter of Patrick Gordon-Walker, who was then Under-Secretary of State and would later become Foreign Secretary. A boy I especially liked was Nick Hawkes, son of the well-known archaeologist Jacquetta Hawkes, who was at the time married to J.B. Priestly. Quinlan Terry, another member, was later to become a well-known architect. He was thought to be a favourite of Prince Charles due to his very traditional designs.

The most senior member of the Club, who was often in charge of the Ark and its inhabitants, was Rodger Harben, son of the first TV cook, Philip Harben. Philip began his cooking career as the cook in the Isobar, the restaurant on the ground floor at the Lawn Road Flats. Rodger used to say he preferred his mother's cooking. When his Dad cooked the family had to endure omelettes, or perhaps donuts, every day for weeks, until Philip had perfected his special recipe. Rodger was also a splendid cook.

Most of the other Theta Club members lived in the Hampstead neighbourhood and close to Lawn Road Flats. Jack and Molly believed in giving their young total freedom and in encouraging their independence and individuality. As a result, there was little adult supervision, but Jack and Molly were nearby in the holidays, in case of any serious problems.

The Ark could accommodate twelve people. The twelve bunks ran the length of the barge on both sides. At the far end was the galley. Each week one of the older members, who had the status of skipper, would be in charge. Every day two people remained behind to tidy and clean the Ark and to buy provisions and cook the evening meal. Everyone else spent the day exploring the Broads in a variety of small craft and half-deckers that belonged to the Club.

A day's excursion can take us as far as Hickling Broad, a wide expanse of mainly very shallow water, where we must be careful to stay in the channels, unless we are sailing in the Norfolk Punt, which has a centre board that can be lifted to enable us to float in just a few inches of water. Horsey Broad is another favourite destination. It is situated close enough to the coast so that we can visit a beautiful and mostly deserted beach after a short walk over the dunes. There is one occasion when I am the only girl aboard. It is early in the year and there are few people about. We picnic on the beach then take off our clothes and plunge into the waves. It is glorious and exciting but also bitingly cold. I have hidden my clothes beside a rock. Finally, we emerge from the sea to find the wind has buried our clothes and they are nowhere to be seen. At this very moment a party of holidaymakers appears on the beach. Mickey eventually finds my clothes, brings them to me and shields me as I quickly pull them onto my soaking wet body, without too great a loss of modesty!

Sailing due north up the River Thurne from our anchorage, which is where the River Bure meets the River Thurne, we come to the village of Potter Heigham. This approach takes us along a stretch of river lined by small holiday bungalows with names like EEEE (For Ease) or Osokosi (Oh, so cosy). In order to visit Potter Heigham there is the added excitement of needing to lower our masts to pass under the low bridge. Sometimes we are able to sail further a-field to visit Great Yarmouth, where the River Yare flows into the North Sea. This takes us two or three days and we have to borrow Jack and Molly's small cabin cruiser to accommodate us at night.

I learn to sail in the Tiddlers and also to skipper the Yare and Bure one design, half-decker sail boats. It is my first sailing lesson that leaves the most vivid impression. Mickey is my teacher. He stands on the bank and pushes me out into mid-stream in one of the Club's Tiddlers. This is a single-handed dinghy with a mast that is far too tall for its tiny hull, which makes it stunningly unstable. I have never sailed before and have no idea how to steer a boat or what to do in relation to the wind direction. We have no safety gear or life jackets, but thanks to my Olympic coach, I am a pretty good swimmer. The dinghy goes round and round in ever decreasing circles, while the sail flaps and jibes as I lurch from travelling with the wind to finding myself with the wind ahead. Mickey stands on the bank splitting his sides with laughter as the dinghy makes a final lurch, tipping me out and ending upside down. After this, I learn how to sail with remarkable speed!

Another member of the Theta Club is Martin Minns. He is a splendid looking fifteen year old and exactly my age, though infinitely older in terms of his experience of life. He has a fine and classically handsome face, a rather distinguished aquiline nose and piercing blue eyes. He is not as tall as my brothers, who are now both well over 6', but is athletic and strongly built. We enjoy each other's company and very often sail together à deux in one of the Norfolk punts.

Early one morning we set off soon after breakfast, together with the flotilla of little boats. On either side of the river are flat pastures where cows graze and bull rushes grow beside the riverbanks. A towpath runs alongside the fields. The open countryside allows a view that stretches from horizon to horizon. There are some areas of mist lying low over the water and a pale early morning sun shines through the patchwork of clouds, but it promises to be a lovely day. There is just enough wind to give us a gentle speed as we reach in a north-westerly direction with the wind across our beam. There are not many other boats on the river, apart from the occasional motorboat carrying holiday-makers who have little understanding of boats or of the rule of the river. We, on the other hand, know that a powerboat must always give way to sail, and have great satisfaction in occasionally, while tacking up river, ramming an unsuspecting motoring holiday maker with our bowsprit when he fails to give way.

We join our fellow sailors for lunch at a predetermined destination. On this occasion we arrive at Horning Broad. We have bread and cheese, fruit and salad and cider to drink. The sun shines. We lie together in the wet grass soaking up the sun while our fleet of small boats is moored at the edge of the Broad. It is the first really hot sun of the season, and we are acutely aware of the newness of life and the joy of being young. Martin takes hold of my hand and I experience a feeling that is exciting, new and most certainly very different to the one I have for my brothers!

We arrive back at the Ark just before dusk. There is an appetizing aroma of beef stew emanating from the galley. The cooks today are Judy Willans, and the gorgeous redhead, Rosalyn, who is the girl Johnny is enchanted by. He says of her, 'She is utterly delicious, from the top of her head to the tips of her toes.' It was during this holiday that he at last finds the courage to hold her hand, while they are walking over the fields together, to collect the daily milk supply with the billycan.

After a supper (that tastes, after our long day in the open air, like food for the gods), of stewed beef and baked potatoes, eaten on the long table that stretches the length of the Ark, with the lower bunk beds as our benches, we clear the dishes away and, as usual, we have a sing-song. There are some good musicians among us and some splendid voices and there is usually someone who can play the guitar. We sing *Green grow the Rushes O*, *On Ilkley Moor Baht 'at*, *Frankie and Johnny*, *If you go to Heaven before I do*, and many others.

Lights out is at about 11.00 and is stipulated by the

weekly skipper, who on this occasion is my brother Mickey. He is a popular skipper because not only is he probably the best sailor in the club and consequently the best teacher, but he is rather less authoritarian than some of the other older boys. When it is time for bed some people go for a skinny dip in the river as the only way to get clean, then we change into our night clothes, climb into our bunks and wriggle down into our sleeping bags. There are no separate boys' and girls' quarters; we all sleep together, dress and undress in public, in one innocent and indiscriminate muddle.

On our way home that year I spend the night at Martin's family home in Hampstead. The Minns have a beautiful house overlooking Hampstead Heath and there is a fine view of the ponds on the Heath from my bedroom window. I am woken early by a large man entering my bedroom. He asks me who I am. I reply, 'I'm Dinny'. 'Fine', he says, 'I'm Anthony'. This is Martin's father. After helping himself to a shirt from his dressing-room cupboard, he leaves me to carry on sleeping. Later that morning I meet Martin's glamorous mother, Margaret, and his two brothers, Jonathan and Patrick.

I leave later in the day to return home to West Byfleet and before I leave Martin kisses me. What an experience it is, that first kiss! The world begins to spin and I find myself transported to some new, unfamiliar land from which childhood has forever vanished. I leave for home with a thundering heart and a feeling that I no longer quite belong to myself.

For the next two years, until we are 17 years old, Martin and I live in each other's pockets. During the holidays he is either staying at my home, where we do country things: paddling our Canadian canoe along the River Wey, riding bikes or hanging out in our large, wild garden. When we are in Hampstead, we walk on the Heath and visit the art collection at Kenwood House, a large neo-classical mansion with lovely views over the wide Heath, which is like a stretch of wild countryside in the heart of London.

I am introduced to paintings by Gainsborough and Reynolds, Constable and Turner. We also attend concerts at Kenwood House. One that leaves a deep impression is with the counter tenor, Alfred Deller, accompanied by the lutenist Desmond Dupré, singing Elizabethan songs. Deller sits very informally at a small table, his music propped up before him while he sings. I have never heard a counter tenor before and find it somewhat disconcerting: such a big manly-looking man with a deep bass speaking voice, yet with a singing voice with the range and clarity of a young boy's.

I learn a lot from Martin and his family about art and culture. They have a privileged life style, particularly considering it is less than 5 years since the war ended. Their cook, Karen, creates wonderful and unfamiliar meals and waits on us at table.

Margaret is a total surprise and wonder to me with her exotic wardrobe and exquisitely manicured appearance. I find it amazing that she can spend a whole hour arranging her coiffure and make up every morning after breakfast. Anthony is only there some of the time. They live a bohemian life style in which both parents are openly engaged in extra-marital affairs. Margaret is busy ironing his shirts one day when she comments to me, 'I think Anthony's latest girlfriend only likes formal shirts. I notice all his shirts have suddenly become pure white.'

A frequent visitor to the Minn's household is a charismatic and beautiful woman called Clement Davenport. Her husband is the distinguished music critic and director, Sir William Glock. He is at the time Head of Music at the BBC. Clement Davenport is a gifted artist who designs and paints the scenery at the Royal Opera House, Covent Garden. She has a very precocious daughter of six, called Oriel, who seems more adept than I am at joining in the adult conversation, as well as organizing all the older people around her in party games such as charades. I remember being rather surprised at how Clement had managed Oriel's early feeding routine. She felt she was too busy to sit and feed the baby herself, so she said she saved time, as soon as the baby was old enough, by suspending the bottle with a cord from a hook in the ceiling, so the baby was able to feed herself. I don't know much about babies at the time, but I do wonder if this is really the best kind of maternal care!

On one occasion, Margaret and my mother are lunching together in London and Margaret asks my mother whether she believes in birth control. My mother is surprised by the question and replies, 'Of course Margaret, but why do you ask?' The question clearly relates to Martin and me. The assumption is that we are sleeping together. In that way we are still so innocent and nothing has happened between us. I presume my mother must know this. She once said to me, 'When a woman first sleeps with a man, she gives her whole self, soul, body and all. It's different for a man, for whom it can be a merely physical experience. It is wiser therefore to wait for this until you meet the man you know you will want to spend the rest of your life with.' Having said this, she always trusted me completely and never inquired about what I was getting up to. Because of her trust, I accepted her words and remained a virgin until I met the man I knew I wanted to marry. In those days this was quite normal: most of my friends, except those with a more Bohemian life-style, remained virgins until they were married.

Martin and I have many wonderful times together. One summer he invites me to join him and his family on their family holiday in Cornwall. They have a house close to the Helford River and Martin has his own Mirror dinghy. We spend many happy hours exploring all the inlets. Above the river, the rolling countryside is thickly wooded with stunted oaks that had been used in other times for the tanning industry. These woods are so dense they are almost impenetrable. We often hear the cacophony made by a family of herons nesting in the oak trees, which sounds like the rattles used at football matches. We spend our days on the water in all weathers and often take part in the dinghy races that seem to be a daily occurrence.

We enjoy one another's company and there is little friction between us. I am totally in love with him and admire his strong physique and masculine beauty. When we return to school we begin exchanging letters almost every day. These letters are somewhat pretentious and prosy and distinctly self-conscious. I think we are both imagining ourselves into some kind of Keats-ian tragedy.

During the next holiday Martin takes me to see his maternal grandfather, Sir Sydney Cockerell, who had at one time been the director of the Fitzwilliam Museum in Cambridge. He is a bed-ridden old man in his '90s with a knitted red night-cap on his head and a white night-shirt. He reminds me of Scrooge. He speaks of all his famous friends and correspondents. There is a letter he shows me from Tolstoy with the address, Yasnaya Polyana as the letterhead. I am mightily impressed. I think there are very few famous people in the world with whom he hasn't had some contact. I'm afraid I have little to say to this distinguished old man and he is less impressed with me than I am with him. As a parting gift, he gives me a letter from Sir Alec Guinness, which I treasure for many years. Martin's paternal grandfather, Sir Ellis Minns, had been Dean of Pembroke College and is equally distinguished.

We have been together for nearly two years when I begin to feel that the relationship with Martin is more intense than I can handle. He is jealous of my other friends, even of my pursuits that don't include him; gardening and playing the violin for example. His response to my withdrawal of attention from him is to go into a deep sulk and a silence that can continue for hours or even days.

I soon become increasingly weary of feeling 'owned' by him. One day I suggest we take a break from seeing one another. We are at my home and he leaves soon after to take the train back to Hampstead. However, in the middle of the night my mother and I hear someone approaching her bedroom through the door that opens onto the balcony (I must have been sleeping in her room at the time). Martin has knocked a chair over and this wakes us both. My mother asks what on earth he is doing. He has come down from London in the middle of the night on his motorbike and has somehow managed to climb up one of the pillars that supports my mother's balcony. Later that night my mother goes down to the kitchen and finds Martin with his head in the gas oven with the gas full on. My mother isn't impressed by histrionics. She simply goes over to the gas stove and turns off the gas.

They talk together for an hour or two and then my mother suggests that he should go home before his parents realize he is missing. It's about 6.00 am when Martin finally leaves. He is about to go without his helmet. My mother hands it to him. He says to her, with a twinkle, 'I wouldn't want to kill myself, would I?' So, this is the end of our relationship; with it comes a great surge of freedom for me. After two years of this intense companionship, my life is my own again. With this relief comes a determination that I will never again allow another person to own me or to take over my life.

Chapter 6

Cranborne Chase

To see the world in a grain of sand,
And heaven in a wild flower.
Hold infinity in the palm of your hand,
And eternity in an hour.

(William Blake)

When I was fourteen I had the opportunity to go to a school that had only been in existence for two or three years. The school's name was Cranborne Chase and it had been founded as the sister school to Bryanston, an unusually free-thinking and liberal boys' public school where both my brothers, and Christopher before them, had distinguished themselves in various ways. I wanted to go to this new school from its inception, but it was only when my Father's older brother, Uncle Jack, offered to pay my fees that it became possible.

I arrive rather late after the start of term. I have gone by train alone from London and take a taxi from Wimborne Station to the school. I arrive at the front door of the Palladian mansion, an impressive 18th century building with Ionic columns and a portico that overlooks extensive grounds and a lake with a small temple at its edge. The stone chapel belonging to the house stands alone on a stretch of the beautifully mown lawns that lie between the house and the lake. At first sight the place seems a little awe-inspiring. I am greeted at the door by the school secretary, Miss Dallas, who leads me to the dining room where the whole school is having lunch.

I am shown to a seat and served with the school dinner. I am particularly struck by the feeling of being at home and completely at ease in this new place. I feel accepted in a way that was never possible in my Cambridge school where I was always something of a fish out of water. I know at once, 'I shall be happy here'. I am scarcely aware, as I take my seat beside a friendly girl called Carol Reynolds who has been asked to shepherd me, of the beautiful proportions of this fine dining room, where we are served rather unappetising post-war meals for the next three years, such as stew and spotted dick with custard. The dining room has a splendid Adams fireplace and beautiful silk wallpaper with a fleur de lys pattern. It is supposed to be one of the most finely proportioned rooms, of its kind, in England.

After lunch I am shown upstairs to my dormitory and my trunk is delivered. We lie on our beds, as was usual throughout our school years, for a half hour's rest. I remember clearly the other girls in that dormitory: my old friend, Jancis Maxwell Eve and Carol Reynolds, whose family live in Portugal. Also, Brigitte Delruelle, a Belgian girl, who has remained a dear and trusted friend to this day. Her father, I later discover, had died of cancer the previous term so, as fatherless daughters we were immediately drawn to one another. Patricia Leaky has a bed near the window. She is teased for wearing powder on her nose and at meals she is made to sit at a separate table in the dining room because she won't eat. I don't think anyone in those days had heard of anorexia nervosa! Finally, there is Jennifer Black, whose parents are friends of my mother. I know already a number of the girls at this school so I never really feel like a stranger or a new girl.

The three years I spend at Cranborne Chase are a time of discovery and also important friendships. It is here, I think, that I begin to experience myself as a separate person; not so much entangled with my mother and her loneliness and unhappiness. We are given an unusual amount of freedom for those days and there is a wide diversity of subjects we can study. I develop what has become a life-long joy in music. I learn to sing and I create our own school madrigal society with some of the boys from Bryanston. Later, I am chosen to sing solo parts in our school choir.

I become suddenly keen on the violin and long to play as beautifully as my friend, Jane Carter. We get up early enough each morning to practice before breakfast. I am struggling my way through a Corelli Sonata while she is giving a fluent interpretation of Mendelssohn's violin concerto in the room next door. How wonderful it would be to play like Janey; at the time it is my dearest wish. She continues to play after we leave school and becomes a successful professional violinist. My violin playing, though it has continued to bring me great pleasure, has never excelled!

There is an air of freedom, new possibilities and excitement about the opportunities for learning. Apart from the standard subjects we have lessons in painting and sculpture, in pottery and woodwork. We are able, on Tuesday evenings, to go over to Bryanston to hear lectures on Humanities and comparative religions as well as special lessons on the Greek philosophers given by the Bryanston headmaster, Thorold Coade. The windows to learning that opened for me at this time have remained important throughout my life: a love of literature and poetry, of wildlife and nature and, of course, an all-consuming love of music.

It is at this school that I first enjoy being chosen as a solo singer. I am asked to take the solo part in our choral concert with Bryanston. I sing the alto solo in Purcell's *Te Deum laudamus.* I remember the words I have to sing in the duet with the bass soloist (sung by the Bryanston master, David Goodfield);

When thou dids't consider to deliver man
Thou didst not abhor
Not abhor the virgin's womb

Singing in front of the whole school felt like a terrifying experience. I told my teacher, Miss Hartnell, that my anxiety about the concert was so great it was keeping me awake at night. She reassured me by saying, 'Just remember that you have been chosen to sing the solo because you are the person who can do it best.' This gave me the necessary confidence and at the concert itself, I felt absolutely fine.

In my final term at the school I take the lead part in an abridged version of the Mozart opera, *The Magic Flute*, which had been adapted for performance in a girls' school. The opera is called *Papageno* and I am to play the starring role as the feathered, light-hearted bird catcher. We perform on the portico in front of the school with parents and Bryanstonians and the rest of the school as audience. It is a triumphant finale to my three years and my singing teacher is keen for me to continue to sing and to make it my career. However, I have been greatly influenced by reading a biography of Albert Schweitzer and have determined that I will train as a nurse and eventually go out to Lambarene to serve as one of Schweitzer's missionary nurses.

Diana as Papagano

My tutor at school is a liberal and erudite man called

Anthony Brackenbury. He has a particular view of education, which is to discover for oneself the wonderful possibilities that life offers and to immerse oneself in these discoveries. He considers passing exams to be a boring necessity, which ultimately is of secondary importance compared to living a full and meaningful life. He reads us a story at the beginning of our year in 3A, when I am fourteen. The story is from China and is about a young girl called Charlemaine. The mantra throughout the story is, 'Make the best of occasion and drink of the brook of the way'. The message of this story is that opportunities only present themselves once in life and if you hesitate or postpone important decisions, the best things in life pass you by.

It becomes my mantra in life also. I take his advice to heart and make the most of every opportunity that school offers, both in relation to the wide range of interests that are available to us, as well as the friendships that I make there, which have lasted a lifetime. Exams have never been an important part of my life, though in everything that I've attempted - nursing, diplomas in music and singing, a BA degree, teaching and finally a training in psychotherapy - I have done well enough to complete the training, to qualify in each faculty and then to work in the different professions.

I was once told by a psychiatrist who read my life story in my hand, that I possessed the quality of persistence and that I would always complete, and succeed in, everything that I attempted. However, I see myself as the tortoise rather than the hare. I plod quietly along and arrive at my destination eventually.

During the summer term when I am 16, I take part in a play by Charles Morgan called *The River Line,* at Bryanston School. I am one of only three girls who are chosen to join the boys' production and we are driven the 12 miles to and from Bryanston by the headmaster himself, Thor Coade. He often comes to our school to teach us and to give memorable sermons at the Sunday services in our school chapel. He also likes to come and visit our head mistress, Betty Galton.

Visits to Bryanston are frequent. I still have a brother, Johnny, at the school and we enjoy meeting one another although he is, at this stage, too shy to get to know any other girls. In a letter home to our mother, which I read some years later, he wrote at this time, 'Dinny is becoming really quite pretty!' That was quite a compliment from a brother who was, on the whole, rather disparaging!

There was one boy at Bryanston who I particularly enjoyed seeing. I made a point, on our weekly Tuesday evening visits, of going to visit him with my friend Annabel Richter, where we could always be sure of finding him; in the pottery. It so happened that when we arrived there every week, he was just completing some magnificent and enormous pot. We found him sitting at the wheel with the wet clay spinning and his strong hands drawing up the sides of the pot and skilfully shaping it 'til it seemed to reach some sort of perfection. He would pause, then cut the pot from the wheel and leave it with other pots that were drying on the shelf as they awaited their biscuit firing. Both Rikki and I were also keen potters at that time and we shared a pottery master with Bryanston: the sculptor, Donald Potter. We stood and watched Dick with admiration and awe as he worked away with total absorption. Dick, (his name is Richard Batterham), was later to become one of the best-known stoneware potters in the UK.

Well, during the *River Line* rehearsals, it is Dick who comes to visit me. He creeps around to the wings while I am waiting to go on stage and we have whispered conversations. He is a good-looking boy with strong, chiselled features and a quietness, thoughtfulness and sincerity that shine from him. He knows, already, without a shadow of doubt, that he will become a potter. He is completely single-minded with respect to his craft and has already developed an amazing mastery. He also has other talents; he is a fine oarsman and rows in the Bryanston eight at Henley. He has a gift also for writing and is at that time the editor of the school magazine, the Bryanston Saga.

We begin to meet at other times and later that summer term he invites me to play in the St Dunstan's tennis doubles match. We are soon meeting to go for walks together. We have country-dancing parties at school; on one occasion that same term we have a dance on the lawn over-looking the lake, with a gramophone playing the music. Dick is also keen on dancing and is my partner at these dances.

Later, during our last term at school, we are invited to a house party by a Bryanstonian who lives in a spacious country house in Worcestershire. We all arrive early and help to prepare the house for the dancing and the delicious spread of food, which is sumptuous after the dull post-war food at school. We dance reels and country dances till we are weary and then go outside to lie under a great wellingtonia tree and tell stories and sing till dawn. It is a romantic ending to our school days. After this party, Dick and I become girl and boy friend and spend many happy times together.

Most memorable is our tour of France and Spain that summer, together with Brigitte (known to us as Bige), and her older sister, Anne, who chauffeurs us in their convertible Chevrolet. We travel to Spain and camp alongside the Mediterranean. We visit the monastery at Montserrat and call on an old friend of my parents, Rosemary Douglas, in Barcelona. We stay in pensions in Saragossa and San Sebastian, finally arriving in the South of France, where we sleep on a rock out in the open, in Cannes, and visit the Picasso pottery and gallery in Vallauris.

We return home via the Dordogne and are lucky enough to make a visit to the original caves at Lascaux before they become closed to the public. We end our tour in Paris and pay a visit to the Louvre, where we discover the original Mona Lisa painting while Anne remains sitting on the Louvre steps reading her detective novel. We stay at Bige's lovely home in Liege on our way home and there we are waited on at table by their haute cuisine cook; I don't think I have ever tasted such exquisite food before. This was the end of the carefree days of school. Life would never be quite so untroubled, sweet and uncomplicated again.

I didn't shine academically at school. As I wasn't one of the more academically gifted there was no pressure on me to apply to university, or to be one of the few high flyers that made it to Oxford or Cambridge. So, I was able to enjoy all the things that school had to offer and I left at 17 with a handful of 'O' levels. As my two best friends, Janey and Brigitte, had already left, I had no desire to remain for 'A' levels, so after leaving school I spent a year at a 6th form college in Guildford, where I took the necessary A' level exams.

Adapting to home life after the richly varied life of school was not easy and I don't remember this as a happy time. I had no friends nearby and my mother lived a very quiet and uneventful life. Few people ever visited our home and we were seldom invited out. I would catch the train to Guildford each morning from West Byfleet station and cycle to the station leaving my bike in a cycle shop nearby. In summer I would often cycle the whole way, which was perhaps 12 miles or so. Much of the route in those days was along narrow country lanes; the smell of newly mown grass and the hedgerows bright with honeysuckle and may made a lovely beginning to the day.

At this time my mother was working as a prison visitor to Wormwood Scrubs so she also had to leave the house early. Every morning she set off on her bike to the station with her little bundle of sandwiches made with her own home-made bread. She visited the young men on remand

and would then visit their families in order to find out about their background and write a very detailed report on the respective boy and the circumstances that had led to him offending. Her sympathy was nearly always with the lad. Circumstances, in terms of family, society or both, had been against these young men from the beginning and my mother felt, with nearly every boy she met, that it was society rather than the boy, who was to blame. Punishment simply confirmed their sense of injustice and disappointment.

The Borstal and prison system acted as a training college for crime, from which it was extremely difficult to extricate oneself. Her understanding and commitment dissuaded many young men from taking this route in life. For some, it was the first time any human being had seen life from their point of view or could recognize in them any potential for a productive life. They were so used to being dubbed 'bad' that many had already identified themselves with 'badness' and a criminal life-style. However, the young men my mother helped were all under twenty. None had yet had a conviction. So, there was still a chance to turn things around.

When I was 15 my mother brought a young man, called Joe, to live with us. He became my adopted brother and was just nineteen years old. Having served his Borstal sentence at the closed Borstal in Portland, there was no longer a family home for him to return to. His parents had both died in the war and he had made no close attachments among the nine families to which he and his seven brothers and one sister had been evacuated.

Joe was tall, well built, dark, and outstandingly good looking. It was lovely for me to have yet another older brother and one who treated me with the greatest gentleness and respect. He fitted very easily into our family and it was, perhaps, a relief for my brothers to have my mother's rather too great involvement in and anxiety about our lives, deflected by someone whose need was so much greater.

At first Joe was with us only when he had leave from Aldershot, where he was completing his National Service. When this was over, Reed House became his permanent home. At the beginning Joe was very dependent on my mother. He became anxious if she was out of sight for even a short time. There were times when he ran away and would ring from a phone box somewhere in London, asking my mother to come at once to find him. She went, whatever the hour, even though (as she never drove again after the war) she had only her bike to get her to the station, a mile away. Her devotion to him was absolute, as was her belief in him. She could see his potential and admired his outstanding intelligence and innate sense of quality.

Eventually, things became easier. Joe felt in a very real sense that he had at last found 'home', possibly for the first time since he had left his parents, at the age of 5. After completing his national service at Aldershot, he studied at home for his 'O' levels, then his 'A' levels, and achieved good enough grades to get him in to Nottingham University. He was popular with the girls and finally fell in love with an adorable girl from Yugoslavia called Maja, who was also a student at Nottingham. He brought her home one summer and we all warmed to this dark, vivacious, girl, so full of laughter and fun. She had a passionate nature and when Maja was around life was never dull!

Joe and Maja married soon after and had a son, called Andrez. We would visit them in their cosy home in Yately, Surrey, and my mother delighted in their absolute wonder and joy in this beautiful baby boy. She would say, 'It's like visiting the holy family.' For Joe, perhaps, this child represented a new beginning and the possibility of a life that would not be scarred by trauma, rejection, suffering and loss. For my mother, there was something profoundly moving in the stability of this lovely family and their home.

Joe's life went from strength to strength. He took a teacher-training course and worked in a school in Yately.

Later, he became the headmaster of a school in London for children who could not be contained in ordinary schools. He possessed a special gift and understanding in relation to troubled children and was able to help those that had been abandoned by the traditional system.

Later still, Joe and Maja established themselves in their beautiful three storey home in Dulwich. When their two younger children, Clare and Nicholas, were growing up and all three were excelling in different ways, Joe was given the job of inspector of schools for ILEA (Inner London Education Authority).

Although my mother didn't live long enough to enjoy his final achievement, every aspect of Joe's life is, in a way, a tribute to my mother's belief and devotion and to her conviction that punishment and incarceration is not the right way to help people who have been let down and traumatised by the society in which they live.

Chapter 7

The New World

We also should walk in the newness of life.

(Romans vi 4)

I had secured my place at St Thomas' Hospital to train as a nurse but had to wait a year before I could begin. When I finished my 'A' levels I was just 18 years old, but one needed to have celebrated ones 19th birthday to start training. I decided to take a year out in the U.S; in order to earn my living there, I took a six-month secretarial course in Guildford and learned shorthand, typing and bookkeeping. Little remains of these skills except the touch-typing which, in this era of computers and email communication, is invaluable.

While I was preparing to work as a secretary my mother had an American friend, Barbara Bosanquet, to stay. Barbara was married to Charles Bosanquet, who owned the beautiful estate of Rock in Northumberland and would later become the first Vice Chancellor of Newcastle University, when it separated from Durham. Barbara had been a Schefflein - an old, originally Dutch family, who were some of the early settlers in New England – and she had a great family of relatives scattered over America. She told my mother that one of her nephews, Fred Osborn, lived in Philadelphia with a family of five children and they were looking for an au pair. They offered to pay my travel fare if I would commit to giving them a year's help.

It doesn't take me long to decide. Within a month I am on board the Cunard Liner, SS Medea, bound for New York. I join a group of young people on board, where we play deck tennis and shuffle board and dance 'til the small hours every night.

I spend much of the voyage in the company of a family

of four sons from Chicago. The eldest, Hal, becomes my partner throughout the trip. He has just left school and is about to take up a place to read chemistry at UCLA. We dance the night away, kiss under the stars and sleep very little. He asks me to marry him, but I am just discovering real freedom for the first time in my life and have no intention of tying myself down so soon. We correspond for a time after the voyage, but his letters are curiously childish and illiterate for someone who is about to begin studying at one of America's great universities.

At dawn, I watch as we approach New York through the mist and see its tall buildings with their myriad lights gradually emerge. This is the beginning of a new life in the New World and I am feeling more keenly alive than I ever remember. I am on my own and I have no family or person close to me to fall back on. I realize that whatever happens in this new life of mine is entirely up to me. This feels both exciting and challenging.

Delli Reed, the daughter of a family friend and the niece of the film director, Carol Reed, meets me in New York and takes me to her family home for the night. The following day she puts me on a train to Maine.

Fred Osborn meets me at Bangor station and I arrive at the Osborn's holiday home, Tranquility Farm, to be greeted by a bevy of small boys and a few older girls. Lunch is on the table and the noise is deafening. It takes me a while to work out which children belong to the Fred Osborn family, as distinct from the many cousins who all spend summers together on this family peninsula. This is a beautiful stretch of land, consisting of spruce woods and narrow rocky beaches, which had been bought by the Schefflein family back in the nineteenth century. When lunch is over I am introduced to my special charge, Charlie, a big, smiling baby of nine months old. He and I will spend the next year and a half in each other's company and will become deeply attached to one another.

That evening we take a flotilla of small boats across the bay to Bar Harbor to watch the film Moby Dick. It has a powerful effect on the three older Osborn sons, Willy, Pelly and Freddy and for the rest of the summer they replay the battle between Captain Ahab and Moby Dick, the great white whale, in the swimming pool.

I soon feel completely at home in this great extended family; not only with Fred, Nancy and their five children, but also with all the cousins, their parents and particularly with Fred's parents, Margaret and Fred Osborn senior. They are infinitely welcoming and generous to me and soon treat me like an additional grandchild.

I gather my duties gradually after my arrival by simply offering to do things: to make beds, wash up after meals, take the children out in one of the boats. I don't remember Nancy ever actually *asking* me to do anything. By the end of the summer I find myself in charge of Charlie, responsible for the cleanliness and tidiness of the log cabins and after a month (the summers in Maine lasted from the end of June until Labour Day in early September), I am also cooking for the family, as the cook suddenly decided to leave.

Between my domestic duties there are sailing races in the many family dinghies, expeditions in the yacht which Fred built, (Nancy Bell), family picnics to Schoodic Point where we enjoy clam chowder, swimming in the Tranquility Farm pool and tennis with Frank Motrill, a professional coach. There are family sing-songs in the evenings when the extended family gathers at the cabin of the Osborns senior.

It is lovely for me when the Bosanquet family joins us that summer in Maine and I enjoy the company of my life-long friend and companion, Clare, daughter of Charles and Barbara. Clare has been a part of my life for as long as I can remember. That summer we enjoy walking, sailing, picnicking and making music together, when my duties as Charlie's babysitter allow. She is as familiar to me as a sister might be, and because we have known each other for so long, we do not have to explain ourselves to one another. We can just be, as we have always been! She is dark, tall and gentle, and possesses a quiet dignity and integrity; she treats everyone, of all ages and social standing, with the same interest and deference.

I have never before been in such an exquisitely beautiful place. The following summer we are there again for the three months of summer when it is too hot to stay in Philadelphia. As all the cabins are filled with friends and family I spend all summer sleeping in a jungle hammock that I sling between two spruce trees near the edge of the sea. From here I can look out over the bay to Ash Island and a variety of long, tree-covered islands, where the only inhabitants are nesting ospreys. On the other side of the bay, known as Frenchman's Bay, is the town of Bar Harbor, just visible in the distance.

The land here is comparatively young. There are a few sandy beaches where the trees, which consist mostly of spruce and pine, extend almost to the water's edge. In the evenings, after the warmth of a summer's day, the sweet scent of spruce resin fills the air and I am rocked to sleep by gentle sea breezes and lulled by the night sounds of croaking frogs, crickets, screech owls and the unearthly calls of the seals from Seal Rock, all of which provide my night music.

I have brought a stack of books with me and read them by torchlight under the canvas roof of the jungle hammock: James Joyce's Ulysses, and books by Faulkner, Hemmingway and Steinbeck. I am woken by the rising sun and go to the main cabin, where Charlie sleeps in a room next to his parents. I quickly dress him and carry him on my shoulders to the place where the dinghy is moored to the dock. We don our life jackets and then I row us out to Seal Rock to see the seals as they lie on their backs on the bare rocks, already sunning themselves. Our arrival surprises them and at a signal from the boss the whole company dives into the sea and we find ourselves surrounded by fifty or more round faces. They are curiously human and inquisitive and their eyes are focused on our every move. These morning expeditions are a lovely, special time before the rest of the family is awake and the furious activity of the day begins once more.

That first summer in Maine is a gentle introduction to my life and responsibilities with the Osborns. We return to Philadelphia in September. The family lives in a large clapboard house in Merion Station, a suburb of Philadelphia. I have a bedroom on the third floor and twelve-year-old Barbara, their eldest child, sleeps in an adjoining room. She is already a confident young woman; in many ways more worldly-wise at twelve than I am at eighteen. Barbara is the one who has authority over the boys when her parents are away. No one dares to disobey her. Charlie, on the other hand, adores her unreservedly and becomes her willing slave.

At first my only duty is to look after Charlie. During the winter months this is not altogether easy and as he suffers from asthma, it isn't possible for him to venture outside when the weather turns cold. And cold it certainly is; no Surrey winter days have ever felt this cold. However, there is almost always a part of the day when Nancy takes over the child-minding so that I can drive off in their car for my various engagements.

I prefer not to have a whole day off but instead to be free to play in the Philadelphia Youth Orchestra on Saturday mornings and on Fridays to attend my violin lessons with Joseph Primavera, the gorgeous Italian conductor of our orchestra, in Philadelphia. Joseph himself plays viola in the great Philadelphia Orchestra. I also learn from him much about life itself and about the behind-the-scenes exploits of a professional musician who spends many months of the year away from home!

On a Tuesday I have a singing lesson with Jane Mortimer, a friend of Nancy's, who has a fine contralto voice. She would like me to take up singing professionally but she also lets me know how hard it is. To get on in the profession, she tells me, you must be prepared to sleep with the conductor or producer. I decide then that such a life isn't for me! However, I feel a greater incentive to practise my violin and singing more conscientiously than I ever have before, now that it is my own hard-earned money that is paying for the lessons.

Nancy trained as a singer at the Juilliard School but married before her career had taken off. She encourages my music and gives me time to practise each day. I think that Charlie must be a long-suffering baby, often playing quietly with his toys under the piano while I warble or saw away at my practice. There are also times of boredom for me. I discover that taking care of a small child, day in day out, when it isn't one's own, can be monotonous. But there are lovely moments too and I am heartbroken to have to leave him when I finally return home.

The following year, Nancy feels that I need a holiday away from the family so she arranges for me to go and stay with her sister, Bibette, who is married to a cowboy called Owen Anderson. They live on a ranch in Montana and own many thousands of acres of dry barren land bordering the Missouri River. I catch the train in Philadelphia and travel across America for 48 hours, in delicious comfort. For much of the time I sit in the observation coach where there is a glass observation tower through which one has a 360-degree view of the passing countryside.

How different it seems from our English countryside where the progression from open countryside with fields of corn, pastures with animals, towns, villages, flat land and hills follow one another in rapid succession. As we approach Pittsburgh we flash by the steel industry chimneys, which belch flames and smoke into the night sky.

From a distance it looks as though we are approaching Dante's Inferno. After a change of trains in Chicago, we pass vast fields of corn for hour after hour as we speed through the American Midwest. We travel through Iowa and North Dakota and then follow the course of the Missouri River for hundreds of miles.

Eventually we arrive at Billings Station in Montana where Owen Anderson, with his cowboy hat, handsome brown face and languid air, is waiting to meet me. He is a veritable Crocodile Dundee. It is a long drive out to his ranch in their battered Land Rover and I have a great welcome from the whole family, including Barbara, who was always known as Bibette, and their two sons, J.O. and Gus. They live in a sprawling one-storey house; the main family room is where everything takes place and is both the kitchen and dining area as well as the sitting room. It is early summer and the weather is beginning to be hot.

The following morning Owen wakes me at 5.00am, the time that every day begins in the Anderson household. As soon as breakfast is over I go out with Owen to catch two horses. We put on their saddles and bridles and away we go, across the dry, featureless acres of his ranch, (Owen has not yet got around to irrigating his land), to round up the steer. This is an all-day event. I have done some riding but riding Western-style is quite different. The stirrups are longer, so one's legs are almost straight by the horses's sides. There is no tension on the reins and none at all on the bit. One steers by gently tapping the horse on the neck with the reins, in the direction in which you want to go. Gentle pressure on the bit is enough to make the horse stop. But the horses need little guiding and are extraordinarily gentle and docile. If I go out alone, as I occasionally do, and forget how to get back (which is easy as there are simply no identifying features to the landscape), then the horse will bring me safely back to the homestead. The only way to navigate one's route is by the sun.

On this first day we ride 'til noon and stop by the Missouri River for lunch. Finally, we find the steer grazing close to the riverbank and Owen begins rounding them up while I help as best as I can. When, finally, the steer are gathered, we begin driving them home. This is a slow business. Owen says; 'You must learn to think like a steer. Learn to move at their pace. If you try to hurry them they'll scatter again.' We arrive home at dusk and drive the cattle into a corral, water the two horses and let them out into the field.

Bibette has the meal ready; never in my life has a meal of roast chicken tasted so delicious. By the following day I am saddle sore and am happy to join Owen on the tractor and to help with cutting the grass and later, baling it into hay. It is a pathetic amount and it takes one whole length of the ten acre field to gather enough grass for a single bale. It is very hot and I sit on the back of the tractor with my very short shorts and watch my legs turning deep brown.

The following day, Owen suggests that we go hunting for antelope with his twelve-year old son, J.O. We fly low over the ranch in his twin-engined Piper Cub plane until we sight a herd of animals on the western perimeter of his land. From above we have a splendid view of the magnificent wilderness of Montana; the wide-open countryside has only a few stunted trees and little green growth. To the north, the great Missouri river snakes its way for as far as the eye can see. There are only a few dwellings visible and only the occasional homestead, for surviving on this dry land is dependent on having several acres for each beast. So Owen's 100,000 acres can only provide a meagre living for his growing family.

Once we have located the antelope we return to the farm. Owen lands the plane and the three of us quickly mount the horses. It takes us about an hour to ride to where we have sighted the animals. Twelve year old J.O. is already a fine shot. He takes aim and one of the antelope falls. Quick as lightening, Owen slits the animal's throat. He loads the antelope onto the back of the fourth horse we have brought with us and we go down to the water's edge beside the swiftly flowing river.

Owen and J.O. find drift wood along the shore and soon have a fire blazing, to cook some of the meat. Owen cuts off some choice parts of the antelope and gives them to me. I eat them with relish. The meat is tender and the taste is different from anything I have known. He calls it 'mountain oysters'. Only after I have enjoyed this delicious al fresco meal does he tell me that we have been eating the antelope's testicles.

I return to Philadelphia after a week but feel I have been away for months; it seems that I have been visiting another planet. I have never before felt so special or such a success as I feel with Owen, Bibette and their boys. They think that everything I do is amazing and exceptional. I sing to them every evening with my guitar and tell them about my life at home and my very modest experiences and achievements. It is as though to them, I am some great celebrity who has just stepped out of the latest popular film.

I have been with the Osborn family for several months when the telephone rings one freezing February morning, while I am preparing the family breakfast. It is my mother, a far away voice from what seems like the other side of the world, to tell me that my wonderful brother, Mickey, had been killed that morning in a car crash on the Barnett bypass.

My world comes to a standstill; I simply continue to function for the rest of that day on automatic pilot. Everything seems unreal and it is impossible to take in the full impact of such a loss. How will the rest of my life be without the person who has been such a vital and constant companion and an essential part of my world for my entire life? Even now, sixty years later, hardly a day goes by when I don't think about him. What would he be like now, as a man in his eighties? What kind of life would he have led? Who would he have married and what children would have become his future? He is in my mind and in my daily world, still so splendidly alive. I think of the words Frances Cornford wrote about the poet, Rupert Brooke, whom she loved deeply, at the time of his death from septicaemia in WW1:

A young Apollo, golden-haired
Stands dreaming on the verge of strife
Magnificently unprepared
For the long littleness of life.

These words are a fitting description of Mickey also.

I leave for home soon after but arrive too late for the funeral. I find my mother lost and bewildered after this bitter blow; the loss of the son who has been for many years the man of the house. He had taken responsibility for all the man-tasks in house and garden; kept the lawns mowed, grew the vegetables, stoked the boiler and chopped the wood and he saw to all household repairs. He looked after his little sister and was in every way my mother's supporter and helpmate. For a time, she doesn't know how she will manage without him and it is Joe who steps into the breach and makes sure that my mother is well cared for.

There is little I can do to help her. One day she consults the Chinese Book of Changes, the I Ching. The hexagram that she receives is the one that is about Holding Together (hexagram 8, Pi). It seems as though she is wanting her two remaining children to stay close to her, at the very time that we are trying to become independent. It is a relief to return to America that summer and I stay with the Osborns until the following January, when I am due to take up my place at St Thomas' Hospital.

Mickey and Bill Masser

John

Mickey

Chapter 8

St Thomas'

But unto you that fear my name shall the sun of
righteousness arise with healing in his wings.

(Malachi iv 2)

I return from America for New Year, 1958, and am due at
the Preliminary Training School (PTS) at St Thomas' on
January 4th. I arrive at the large country house in Godalming
where we are to spend our first introductory weeks,
brimming with confidence and with a fairly pronounced
American accent.

I am a little late and am met by Miss Gamlin, a
formidable and rather handsome middle aged woman who is
the principal of the training school. I walk up to her with a
greeting and hold out my hand to shake hers. She gives me
an icy glance and says, 'We don't shake hands here, nurse.
Put your hands behind your back.' I feel very firmly put in
my place and my American confidence seems to disappear
like a puff of smoke.

The majority of the probationers (with the exception of
four or five) have come straight from school. Most have
arrived from rather strict girls' schools, so the military-style
discipline is, possibly, not as great a shock for them as it is
for me. Even at school, I had never encountered such rules,
discipline and restrictions as we had to accept during the
next ten weeks. After almost two years of freedom in
America, and my own independent life, it comes as a severe
shock to be treated as someone less than human. I think
Miss Gamlin has made a mental note, after our initial
encounter, to knock all the cockiness out of me and reduce
me to an amenable and obedient subject.

We are told, constantly, that the nurses at St Thomas' are

the best in the world and that they are regarded not only as totally professional but, in the eyes of their patients, as angels. The dictum of Florence Nightingale is that every patient, no matter how ill or old or difficult, must be treated like an 'honoured guest'. The treatment we receive, however, is often harsh and demeaning, so we are certainly not taught by example!

During these early weeks we learn through lectures and demonstrations the basic ingredients of nursing and nursing procedures: we learn how to give a bed bath, how to admit a new patient, tooth-comb for nits, bandage an injured limb and apply sterile dressings; these procedures we practice on one another. We also have lectures on the fundamentals of anatomy and physiology.

We perform household tasks and are taught how to sweep a floor and make scrambled eggs. I find it both extraordinary and amusing to be taught these things. One early morning, while sweeping the demonstration room floor with Hester Pleuger (who becomes a life-long friend, and was later to become Lady Hester Touche, as the wife of her distinguished husband, Sir Anthony), she asks me why I want to take up nursing. This is a serious question; she will become an outstanding nurse. Already she is showing signs of being the person in our set who will come out top, to receive the gold medal. My answer is intentionally flippant; perhaps I want to tease her a little. I reply, 'because I want to marry a doctor.' Perhaps I am being more serious than I know, because that is exactly what I do, although not before I have finally qualified as a Nightingale.

To my surprise, I pass out of the PTS with flying colours in spite of Miss Gamlin's very evident dislike of me. I have my second interview with the matron, Theodora Turner, a most delightful, humorous and human person and I know, from now on, that things will be fine.

My first interview had also been a positive one and I warmed to her from the first moment of our meeting.

Theodora is an unassuming person and has the gift, even from her exalted position, of putting one completely at one's ease. In my initial interview, which I had before leaving for America, I remember her comment as I was shown into her room; 'Ten 'O' and 'A' levels you say, well she will certainly have a place.' So, I had a remarkably relaxed interview as a result. I remember rather a long wait outside matron's office before it was my turn to go in and being totally absorbed in reading *Dr Jekyll and Mr Hyde;* perhaps not an altogether inappropriate book.

We soon discover that the 'angel' persona of the Nightingale nurse carries with it a remarkably dark shadow and our treatment varies tremendously according to the sister of the ward. Some of the sisters are certainly wonderful nurses but are quite sadistic when it comes to their junior nurses. It is important to have a significant life outside the hospital in order to have some sense of proportion. Theodora seems to take one's rather varying ward reports with a pinch of salt, recognizing that some of the sister's assessments are far from objective.

The years at St Thomas' are important as an introduction to a world so very different from my childhood world of privilege and tolerance. It is the first time, for me, of having to stick to rules that have reference to life and death situations. It is no longer a matter of whether or not one feels like doing something. We are small cogs in a great wheel and if one cog is faulty the whole machine is at risk.

The first experience of working on the wards after the somewhat artificial setting of the PTS, is for me, a real awakening. The patients in Charity Ward, a women's medical ward, are mostly lovely, courageous and witty Lambethians. (St Thomas' is in the London borough of Lambeth). I have never met, let alone come close to, people like this before, closeted as we are in our middle class lives. They never complain about their sufferings and they make us laugh with their richly, pictorial language and earthy jokes.

I think especially of Mrs Jones who has advanced rheumatoid arthritis. She can no longer walk and her hands and fingers are like bunches of bananas. She is in almost continual pain. But her infectious laughter and indomitable spirit are an inspiration. After she is discharged, I visit her at her house in Lavender Hill, where she gives me tea. I don't know what support she has at home but her stoicism certainly affects me and makes me aware of how spoiled my life has been. I find myself thinking less about how I am feeling - whether I am tired, fed up, in a bad mood or suffering from headache or exhaustion. One's personal little woes seem to get washed away in the great tide of other people's suffering.

The early days on the wards are totally exhausting but also, for me, exhilarating. We are up at dawn, when the nurses' coach collects us from our nurses' home, Chelsea Court, on the Chelsea Embankment, and takes us to the hospital in time for some breakfast. We are due on the wards at 7.30 am when for half an hour we help the night staff prepare the 30 patients in the old Nightingale ward, for the day. At 8.00 am on the dot, just as Big Ben is striking, Sister says prayers and all the nurses go down on their knees. How often I long to just curl up where I am and sleep and how we envy the patients, lying so snugly in their warm beds! Someone asks me, one day, what would happen if we were late on duty. I am astonished at the question. Being late is, simply, impossible. No one has ever even considered it!

We work until 9.00 pm with a three hour break at some point in the day, either in the morning or the afternoon. While on duty we are not allowed to sit down. Even if there is nothing to do, it is important to appear busy. In reality, we are working flat out and there are only moments of leisure when we can enjoy the view of the Houses of Parliament and Big Ben across the great River Thames; 'I do not know much about gods; but I think that the river is a strong brown god, sullen, untamed and intractable.'(T.S.Eliot). These lines came to me as I grew to love that great river and its continuous 24 hour a day traffic. What an inspiration, to be able to enjoy one of the loveliest of views in London as we pass through the sluice emptying bedpans!

The few hours off during the day are not enough to return to our nursing home, so we spend them close to the hospital. There is a swimming pool we can use opposite the hospital in Riddell House. I sometimes wander along the road to the Festival Hall in my uniform and listen to the rehearsal of the evening's concert, pretending that I am the nurse on duty. Noone ever questions me and I come and go as though I belong there.

Sometimes, wearing mufti, we take the bus into the West End to look at the shop windows (we don't have enough money to buy clothes), and usually the bus conductor recognizes that we are nurses (is it due to our general look of exhaustion or our flat-heeled Oxford shoes and lack of make-up and glamour?) and refuses to charge us a fare.

There are restrictions. For instance, we are not allowed to stay out after 10.00 pm without a special pass, which are limited to two per month. We are supposed to lead an altogether celibate life; no man is ever allowed into our rooms. When a man is discovered playing his guitar in my room after midnight one night, I am threatened with expulsion. When I explain that it was my brother, John, I have to supply some proof of his identity.

Strange though it may seem, I have never in my life experienced such a sense of freedom. These boundaries are a part of the job and the absolute discipline it requires. It is something I have *chosen* to belong to and the patients are the reason for our personal limitations. One spring evening, I find myself running and leaping down Royal Hospital Road as though I am experiencing true freedom for the very first time. What an irony; it's something I can't adequately explain, how this sense of liberation coincides with the greatest outer discipline and confinement that life has ever presented me with!

I make new friendships which last a life time. There is music. The STH choir is excellent and is conducted by Dykes Bower whose brother is the organist at St Paul's Cathedral. There is the STH orchestra, which has been conducted by Sir Colin Davies and is in my time conducted by Mike Rawlins, a medical student who is to become an eminent pathologist.

I have a friend called Colin Small who has just started a travel company called Murison Small. Colin's home becomes my home from home in London. He is a good musician and he accompanies me while I sing. He also has a regular gathering of amateur singers at his house; we sing madrigals together. I often spend the night at his family home in Shepherd's Bush and sleep in the spare bed in his mother's room. We spend holidays together at his company's chalet in Villars, Switzerland, and in a villa in Blanes, Spain, in the summer. These are wonderful holidays, spent with other young single friends. I could never otherwise have afforded them on the meagre £700 per annum which is our nurses' pay.

One day in December 1959, when Christmas is approaching, we are rehearsing, as we do every year, for the annual nativity tableau. Robert Gilchrist, a fine musician, is our conductor. There is an additional musician this year who is a guitarist. His name is David Crockford.

When the rehearsal is over we have all planned to go down to the psychiatric wing in the basement known as Scutari, to share a bottle of wine. David and I go ahead and find ourselves sitting alone and talking shyly. David is holding a box of Black Magic chocolates his mother has donated for the occasion. He is already a qualified doctor and has travelled from Wolverhampton, where he is working round the clock in his first surgical house job.

It is some time before the others join us, but something

has happened between us. The following spring I receive a note from David in my pigeon hole outside Matron's office, saying, 'I will be sailing with my father on the Medway on Saturday; let me know whether you can/can't come.' Not the most romantic invitation I have ever received, but the invitation intrigues me. I go to see my friend, Andrew Henderson, who had originally introduced me to David. At the time Andrew is a patient in Albert medical ward, suffering from glandular fever. I ask him what this invitation could mean; it is a big one for a little probationer nurse to be invited to sail, and visit the home, of a qualified doctor. To us, doctors were gods. And what's more, a doctor who is the son of the secretary of the STH medical school, Dr Allen Crockford, a name to conjure with. He is to the medical students what matron is to us. In reply to my anxious query Andrew replies, 'Oh, I expect they are just wanting a crew.' And so I go. It is the beginning of what is to become the most important chapter of my life.

Part Two

Chapter 9

Marriage

> *Let me not to the marriage of true minds*
> *Admit impediments. Love is not love*
> *which alters when it alteration finds,*
> *Or bends with the remover to remove:*
> *O no! it is an ever-fixèd mark,*
> *That looks on tempests, and is never shaken;*
>
> (Shakespeare: Sonnet 116)

I had already learned something about David from his closest friend, Andrew Henderson, who I came to know through singing in the Thomas' choir. Andrew had spoken of David with great fondness and admiration, saying that he had outstanding qualities as a human being and was someone who seemed to have unassailable integrity. Andrew clearly thought that David was in every way an exceptional person.

Andrew himself had a highly-gifted, complex and multi-faceted personality. He was often baffled by his own complexity; nothing for him was ever straightforward. Dr. Allen Crockford - who was to become my father-in-law - said that Andrew was the most brilliant student he had ever had at St Thomas'. He arrived from Cambridge with a double first in Natural Sciences and then managed to fail his final medical exams at STH because he answered the questions from the point of view of an established doctor, instead of the humbler standpoint of a medical student! Andrew found David's uncomplicated approach to life profoundly reassuring. I used to think of them as Hamlet and Horatio; Andrew was, of course, Hamlet. They certainly had a lot in common!

After a little hesitation I accept David's somewhat abrupt invitation. His parents live in an oast house in Kent, where they have a large and beautiful garden. Both are passionate gardeners. David meets me at Borough Green Station. The entrance to their property, from the garage, takes us through their enormous fruit and vegetable garden where there is a sense of abundance and fertility. It makes me realize why we refer to Kent as, 'The Garden of England'. I see an elderly man in overalls among the cabbages and assume it is the gardener. David introduces me to Dr. Crockford, who greets me warmly saying, 'What a terrible tragedy about the death of your brother, Michael.' Of course, I warm to him immediately. Mickey had been killed just months before he was due to begin his medical studies at St. Thomas'. He had been interviewed and accepted by Dr. Crockford while studying medicine at Cambridge; Dr. Crockford accepted many students not just for their academic prowess but also for excellence in other areas, in particular, sport or music. He used to say that if a young person had the discipline to attain excellence in another field they would also have the discipline necessary to become a doctor. So, the fact that Mickey was a fine athlete and a rowing blue had been in his favour.

Having passed through the vegetable garden, we walk through an archway cut into a very tall laurel hedge that divides the gardens of Dr. and Mrs. Crockford. Her domain is the flower garden and what a totally amazing garden it is. Roses flower in abundance, the scent of the syringa blossom hangs in the air and a rock garden that could have been conceived by the RHS, lies in one corner.

We wander into the kitchen where Mrs. Crockford is preparing lunch. She also welcomes me warmly and I am made to feel immediately at home. After a meal of soup and bread and cheese we set off for the Medway at Rochester, where Dr. Crockford's 25ft Bermuda-rigged yacht, Tai Ping, is moored. We sail out into the Medway, the sunlight sparkling on the wake, as we reach out into the channel with a fresh breeze abeam. We continue in the estuary until we are within sight of the open sea, with Rochester Castle high above us on the port side and a fair wind, which gives us a sense of heady speed. I feel at ease with David and his father and they treat me with an old fashioned courtesy, so different from the way I have been used to being treated by my brothers at home. Dr. Crockford invites me to take the helm. It may be the first time I have sailed a yacht, rather than the half-deckers we were used to at the Theta Club. I borrow David's sailor hat to keep the hair out of my eyes and any sense of shyness I may have felt melts away.

Tea awaits us when we return to the Oast House. David then drives me back to the station to return to Thomas'. It has been a memorable day. I don't expect anything to follow but there is something about David, his personality and his very presence that I have found somehow familiar and reassuring. Although we haven't yet spoken much together, I have a sense of being relaxed in his company; of not needing to be anything other than who I am. It has been a day that has made me strangely happy.

I am aware of something beginning to stir. At the time I am still deeply involved with Andrew. We have never really been girl and boyfriend but there is a connection between us that feels like a recognition. We share each other's poetry and speak of things I have never spoken of with any other person. He invites me to his lodgings and we sometimes sing together. Finally, it is Andrew who introduces me to David.

On one occasion we spend a night together on Dartmoor in Andrew's tent. I remember saying to him, 'If you do not want us to be together, then I don't want to sleep with you,' and he respects this. He is never straight-forward about anything and his relationship to the outdoors, nature and perhaps also to women, is complex and tortuous. As we walk in the dying light that evening, with the sun setting over the moor and the landscape radiant with the colours of the setting sun, Andrew's comment is, 'Oh, what a phantasmagoria of clouds,' and he stoops down to view them from different angles as though he is about to capture them in a painting.

He is, indeed, a very fine water-colourist: we are lucky enough to possess a great number of his paintings. But my feeling is, 'Why can't you just enjoy it!' To me, his comment seems out of tune with everything that is young and new and vital. On the train, going back to Thomas' the following day, the thought comes to me, 'With Andrew, life would always be complicated, confusing and difficult but with David, there would be happiness.' It was still a long time before David and I were really even thinking about being together, but somehow, I already knew.

So, after this initial meeting with David at his home, there are occasional meetings in London, further visits to his parents' home and more afternoons aboard Tai Ping. I feel supremely happy in his company. He is a tall man - 6' 3''- very blond and is always refreshingly honest and straight-forward. At first he is shy and not very used to being with a girl. I love the sound of his voice and everything about him seems enabling. When he hugs me I feel totally embraced, not just physically; everything I am is somehow contained in that embrace. Noone has ever before made me feel so totally at ease and accepted, blemishes, shyness and all.

While we are getting to know each other that first summer, he invites me to join him and his father as they sail Tai Ping from Rochester to Portsmouth. I am with them for the final leg; when we reach Portsmouth, David and I travel back to London and I have to return to Thomas'. On the train we have a carriage to ourselves. We take the opportunity to enjoy some uninterrupted hours together, perhaps for the first time. He looks at me, into my eyes, and

I know that his kisses are altogether different from anything I've known before. As he holds my face between his two hands he scrutinizes my sunburned and unmade-up face and says, 'You're not very beautiful, are you?' I maybe return the compliment; certainly, he is not conventionally handsome.

It is a strange communication between lovers, and yet, I feel strangely reassured by it. For one thing, I realize that when he *does* compliment me, it is the truth, absolutely. But also, it seems that he is loving me now in a way that is independent of my looks; the looks will, in time, fade, but he loves me for who I am. It feels like a more enduring way to love and for me it is the same. He is not as handsome or as strongly built as my two brothers, but he has qualities that feel, to me, totally real and dependable. That train journey is when it all began and I am already completely in love with him. None of the many people I had known before who had loved me and been loved by me had held me so completely and moved me to such depths. After this holiday, I know that David is the man I want to marry. Perhaps he knows it too, but it takes him a little longer to trust that feeling.

Johnny comes to visit me one day in the flat I share with three other nurses in Winchester Street, Pimlico. He asks me how one can know that the person you love is also the one you should marry. I say, 'It's when you realize that you can't live your life without that person.' That is how certain I was beginning to feel about David.

David is now a middle-grade surgical registrar in Wolverhampton and working crazy hours, so our meetings are brief and infrequent. He drives to London perhaps once or twice a month and we have fleeting times together while he stays with Andrew at his flat in Pitt Street. I wait for his letters with increasing impatience and am tormented by longing for him.

It is nearing the end of my training at Thomas' when I

go to stay with the Crockfords on the first free day I have after Christmas (1961). David and I sleep in the two roundels at the far end of the Crockford's beautiful oast house. Our rooms are next door to each other. David comes into my bed first thing in the morning and says that his best friend and confidant in life has been God; that he converses with him and confides in God all his deepest thoughts. Now, he says, he has found someone else to be a companion to this deep part of him; it is a first for him to feel this close to another human being. It is then that he asks me to marry him. Oh, yes, yes, yes! How happy I am, and I have never been more certain about anything in my entire life.

Later that day, as we drive over the Dartford Bridge on our way to visit Tai Ping, who is at the ship yard undergoing her winter maintenance, we tell David's parents. We are travelling up the A40 in his father's old, battered Morris Minor station wagon and we sing the song 'Oh no John, no John, no John, no', together, with special emphasis on the final verse:

> *'Oh madam if you are so cruel*
> *And that you do scorn me so,*
> *If you will not be my lover,*
> *Madam will you let me go.'*

Oh no John, no John, no John no.

In spite of our exaggerated expression in that last verse, they don't pick up on our hint. So eventually we tell them that we are to be married and my lovely future father in law's response is, 'Ah, so the old man's popped the question at last!' So, they have clearly been expecting it.

We celebrate that night and my mother-in-law to be treats me, for the next months until our wedding, with the deference due to a princess. I must be served first, have the choicest parts of every dish and go first through every door.

She said she wanted me to know how special I was, in contrast to her own experience; she told me that on being introduced to her future mother-in-law, Dad's mother's reaction was to burst into tears! I have never felt so celebrated and special in my life before.

My time at Thomas' is nearly at an end. No more than one week after we become engaged, my training is finished. On January 4th, 1962, I become a qualified Nightingale nurse. A few days before, I had applied for a scholarship at the Guildhall School of Music. I manage to win the scholarship, which is enough to cover my singing and violin lessons as well as the three year training needed to become a teacher, performer and professional singer. The scholarship is extraordinarily generous by today's standards and is enough for David and me to live on in London during the first six months of our marriage. The new term has already begun so I begin my training immediately after leaving St Thomas'. What a very different world I suddenly find myself in.

But first, those of us who are now leaving St Thomas' must go to Matron's office to say a final farewell to our lovely matron, Miss Turner. I have always liked her affirming presence and delicious sense of humour. Some of the ward sisters, perhaps disappointed with their single state, could be merciless and punishing but on previous occasions when I have been sent to matron for various misdemeanours, she has been gentle and humorous. On every occasion, I got off lightly.

I am full of apprehension because I am not leaving to take up nursing, but to marry and also to change career tack completely. I feared some comment like, 'So, another wastage!' To my great surprise, Theodora smiles at me appreciatively and says, 'So, the Nightingale is fledged and is about to burst into song.' I feel like singing right there and then. It seems that this lovely woman is sending me out into the world, to a very different way of life, with her blessing. Somehow, this seems to matter a great deal. Our meetings have been few and infrequent but each one seems to have an abiding effect on me.

And so I am now free to sing and to devote all my days to music. The change from the rigidity of Tommies, where speaking with a doctor in a public place is not allowed unless it is concerned with work, is at first overwhelming. In contrast, one bumps into entwined couples round every corner at the Guildhall. It feels liberating and totally refreshing to be in this vital place filled with young and gifted musicians. The notes and chords and trills of music practice resound throughout the building.

In fact, it isn't totally unfamiliar to me because I have been having singing lessons there with Walther Grüner for most of my time at St Thomas' and have somehow managed to work this around my free afternoons. I have already been attending his lieder class and have met many of his gifted students; the most gifted among us is Benjamin Luxon who was to become well-known, particularly as a wonderful lieder singer. In this class I am also with Jenny and Ian Partridge, a brother and sister who perform together; Jenny accompanies me for my scholarship audition. What a wonderful musician she is! It is probably largely due to her playing that I am successful in winning the scholarship! Gill Gomez, a beautiful soprano who would also become widely known, is another gifted singer who I later get to know well. In this company I very soon learn where I stand in the scheme of things!

Singing is now no longer a hobby, it is to be my profession. A very different atmosphere and expectation prevails. Walther Grüner teaches us in the German style: every lesson is like a mini master class and we regularly attend each other's lessons. In this way we learn from one another. It can be hard at times, however. Grüner is teaching us that being a professional musician is not a bundle of fun; it is a hard discipline and requires total dedication, self-confidence and stamina as well as the ability to manage rejection and disappointment without losing heart. He makes us work; he requires perfection and we are frequently reduced to tears. His praise is rare, but wonderful when it comes. Above all, we know that we wouldn't be there, and we certainly wouldn't be his students, unless he had believed in us. We soon realize that the tougher he is in his criticism the more he believes in our ability to survive in the profession. There are occasional students in the lieder class who don't have the necessary talent or musical ability. With them, he is always gentle and kind. It is clear that the more he pushes us, the more he feels we are capable of.

I remember one glorious occasion when I am having a lesson at Grüner's house in Finchley Road. Ben Luxon is also there. I am singing an aria from Bach's St John's Passion. For once, Walther is happy with my performance and says to Ben, 'What did you think of that?' Ben replies, 'It was wonderful.' Then Walther says to us both, 'She will make the grade,' which is the highest compliment he could give us. With his belief in me I now feel that I could achieve anything!

Not long after this lesson, I have my first professional engagement. I am to sing Rossini's Petite Messe solennelle in Leicester. This is a somewhat operatic work and requires a big mezzo voice with a wide range. Walther prepares me for this concert as though I am a racehorse preparing for a race. It has to be perfect; there can be no room for error. He tells me that for a performance one must know the piece not just 100%, but 125%, to allow for the effect of nerves. I have never worked so hard at anything in my life. Beforehand I am so anxious that our wedding, which is to take place two weeks after the concert, is almost overshadowed by this huge event. However, when I begin to sing during the concert and I see the smiling appreciative faces of the audience instead of Grüner's shaking head and critical looks, all my nerves disappear. I know that from now on all will be well. The concert is a success and I enjoy every moment of it. I feel that I have well and truly embarked on my new career.

However, what of our marriage? I suppose that compared with today's world we know each other so little. We have been together on David's infrequent visits to London and at other times when we stayed in each other's family homes. Also, I know and love David and how he thinks and feels from his letters that are such a source of joy for me. When I find one of his letters, written in his fine, spiky handwriting, in my pigeonhole outside matron's office, that day is indeed a red letter day! David is in my mind every hour of every day.

On one occasion he invites me to stay with him in his lodgings in Wolverhampton. It is the first time we have been on our own together for an entire weekend. But David is clear that he wants us to wait 'til we are married before sleeping together. While I am there, David's sister and brother-in-law, Jill and Jimmy Walker, come to stay. They are on their annual visit from Barbados with their baby Charlotte, who is eighteen months old. They bring a brace of grouse, which I cook for them, and afterwards I enjoy feeding baby Charlotte. I think that Jill and Jimmy assume we are already living together because they never tell David's parents about this meeting. In those days, it was still unusual to have a full sexual relationship before marriage.

The following day David takes me across the border to the Welsh mountains. We climb, visit a waterfall and lie together in the late afternoon sun. I know now with every single part of me that David is the person I want to be with for the rest of my life. Being with him feels like the most natural thing in the world and there is an easiness and wonderful contentment in our togetherness. There is also a feeling of mutual recognition in our conversations and an ease and gentleness in our silences.

David tells me he has never been able to speak with anyone before with such ease and intimacy, with the exception, perhaps, of Andrew. He isn't close to either of his two older sisters, Meg and Jill, and there has been no real intimacy with either of his parents, even though he and his father have spent so many holidays sailing together. Talking simply hasn't been a part of the family tradition; David has been something of a loner all his life. So sharing thoughts, feelings and life experiences with someone is, for him, something strange and new. These early days of getting to know one another are like a voyage of exploration. It feels to me like a great wonder; sometimes I question whether I can hold so much happiness, or indeed, even believe it to be real.

Our wedding day is planned for May 26th, 1962. My mother is hosting the wedding at our home, Reed House, and the marriage service takes place in our local church in Pyford, where I was christened and which is famous for the fact that the poet, John Donne, was once its minister.

Our small Thomas' choir has agreed to sing for us with our friend and conductor, Robert Gilchrist. When they ask us what music we would like it is suggested that they should sing Bach's *Sleepers Wake* because David has a reputation for falling asleep in the front row, during his medical lectures. However, on his wedding day he manages to stay awake and the choir sings for us *Jesu, Joy of Man's Desiring*. Our vicar, Mr. Church, has prepared us beforehand and has emphasised the sacredness of our marriage vows as well as the recognition that marriage is one of the most important, as well as the most difficult undertaking of any lifetime.

It is the coldest May day on record so I wear some pyjamas under my wedding dress, which I have made myself with the sewing machine given to me by my future parents-in-law. I have also made my trousseau as we had little money between us at the time. It is a simple wedding;

my brother, John, gives me away and only close friends and relatives are invited. The reception at Reed House is held mostly outside, with the rhododendrons in full bloom and the garden looking at its best.

While the guests arrive David and I stand together in the hall and greet everyone as they queue to shake our hands. When it comes to the turn of my old friend Richard Batterham, who is already an established potter by that stage, David holds his hand, roughened with the daily routine of turning pots on the wheel, looks at him for a long time and then says, 'You must be the potter.' Then it is the turn of beautiful Virginia Greenshields, who had been the love of David's life for many years. She also holds my hand for a long time and then says, 'Look after him well.' It is at our wedding that she meets her future husband, another doctor, Peter Bedford; they are still married today.

We cut the cake; then there are speeches. Uncle Jack, my father's eldest brother and another tall man of nearly 6'6', gives a lovely speech wishing us well and praising David. He also says that he hopes that Dr. Allen Crockford can be a father to me as I lost my own father so early in life. He did, indeed become a wonderful father to me and I became deeply fond of him.

David and I finally take our leave amid the confetti and cheers and drive to The Lamb Inn at Hinton, near Salisbury, in David's ancient Morris Minor: registration EYA. This is where we spend our wedding night. I had made an elaborate nightie and flouncy dressing gown for our honeymoon, but these prove largely irrelevant! We dine in the pub and retire to our room, both of us exhausted after the long day. That night I lose my virginity and so does David, although nothing really happens until the following night. There is fumbling, trepidation and wondering how it is meant to be, but in the end, the bloody patch in the bed is proof that we are now truly husband and wife. I feel that I am at last a whole woman and no longer just a girl!

We spend our honeymoon in a log cabin on the banks of the Helford River, in Cornwall. It is a small dwelling that was created many years before by Bobby Warrington-Smyth (by now a widow) and her husband, Bev. It has no legal presence but is well hidden among a forest of small oak trees, so its existence has never been discovered. It is a time like the beginning of the world and we are Adam and Eve, entirely alone in our little world. There is no running water or electricity and David has to chop down trees to create logs for our fire. We cook on the open fire and draw water from the rain butt.

Moored at the water's edge is Campion, the boat that Beverly Warrington-Smyth had made. It is a small sailing boat with a single gaff-rigged sail and an outboard motor. As we are so far up the river we have to time our comings and goings according to the tides because at low tide the river dries out completely. It is a long way from London and the world of work. We are learning about surviving without any visible signs of civilization and we are also learning about the realities of being together for 24 hours a day.

We live naked, when the weather is fine, and discover our bodies through one another. When we visit Bobby's house we experience the excitement of having our first bath together and also the delicious joy of swimming naked, as though we are the first man and woman to discover these delights! We love the day to day-ness of living together; catching mackerel to cook on the fire, chopping logs, washing in a bucket of water, chugging around the river and, when the wind allows, sailing in our small craft and exploring Frenchman's Creek and the haunts of Daphne du Maurier. We make love in the open air and visit lovely Bobby when we need other companionship.

We decide to go further afield and sail to Falmouth. We have a tent and David finds us a suitable campsite in a field alongside the estuary. He starts to make a fire, prepares to cook our supper and asks me for the matches. But there are no matches; I have forgotten to bring them. This is a major disaster. I am somehow entirely to blame for this oversight. It seems as though we have hit a reef, a total catastrophe. Everything collapses. Our whole world is about to fall apart. I am totally bewildered as to what has given rise to this absolute disaster.

I see a house in the distance with a single light burning. I trudge over fields, jump over ditches and eventually arrive at a farmhouse. I explain that we are camping at the water's edge and have no way of making a fire, and that we have already tried rubbing two sticks together, without success. I don't tell the farmer that our marriage has almost collapsed after only one week, for want of a box of matches! He gives me the matches and all is well - we light our fire, cook our mackerel and retire to bed in relative harmony, but I realize how fragile a thing this new relationship is. In retrospect, I am aware of how entirely unused to any real intimacy David has been all his life and that being with another human being for 24 hours a day has been more than he can handle.

The rest of the honeymoon passes without mishap. The magical essence of Otter Lodge stays with us and every successive year we spend our holidays there; a tradition which continues when the children are little. There is something so refreshing about this beautiful place.

Our wedding day

Chapter 10

Married Life and Singing

> *My heart is like a singing bird*
> *Whose nest is in a water'd shoot.*
> *My heart is like an apple tree*
> *Whose boughs are bent with thick- set fruit.*
> *My heart is like a rainbow shell*
> *That paddles in a halcyon sea;*
> *My heart is gladder than all these,*
> *Because my love is come to me.*

We have rented a flat in Wandsworth, London, at No. 14, All Farthing Lane, at the exorbitant price of four guineas a week. David is studying for his FRCS, (Fellow of the Royal College of Surgeons), so he is once again a full-time student, which means that for the first six months of our marriage we have a chance to get to know each other. Thanks to my generous scholarship it is possible for David to engage in full-time study, whereas many of his contemporaries have to manage their studies around a normal working day. David sits at his desk, putting in almost eight hours of study a day, and I commute to The Guildhall, which at that time is situated in Blackfriars, only a short distance from St. Pauls Cathedral. I go to a local church in our road each morning for my singing practice. We are both engrossed in our separate studies and we are also discovering about married life!

I remember it as a time of gentle discovery and of welcome visits to our parents' homes at weekends to escape from London; sometimes to Reed House, but mostly to Kent, to the Oast House, and in summer to crew on Tai Ping. I buy food and become adept at discovering delicious meals using the cheapest cuts of meat: breast of lamb, lamb's liver and scrag end of neck, bought on my way home from the Guildhall. I enjoy scanning the cookery books for new recipes. It is like a childhood game of playing mothers and fathers: everything so exciting and new.

For David, the close proximity to another person demands a long and difficult adaptation. There are times when he withdraws so deeply into himself that I'm unable to reach him. He spends all his free hours at his desk and studying becomes a means of escape. At those times, the only way I can make contact with him is to leave little notes on his desk, just to remind him that I am still around.

There is a time, maybe three or four months after we are married, when his back, which has always given him trouble, gives way completely. He is hospitalized and for two or three weeks lies in a ward in Thomas', on traction. I visit him every evening on my way home from the Guildhall. His back problem may be due to hours of sitting without any real exercise, but it also feels like a way of escaping a situation in which he is feeling increasingly claustrophobic. I find this hard but also, to some degree, understand it, and am not disheartened. The fact that I am fully occupied and entirely stretched with my studies, daily singing and violin practice, as well as with the preparation for professional engagements in London, is comforting. Also, I know in some part of me that in time, things will become easier for David.

These six months are like a rehearsal for the real business of marriage. David is successful in passing his FRCS, an exam that is necessary before he can become a middle grade surgical registrar. Now he needs to find a job, so he answers an advertisement for a surgical job at the Victoria Royal Infirmary in Leicester where his friend, James Hadfield, is a brilliant senior surgeon. It is one of the busiest surgical units in the country. James's wife, Anne, was also a Tommie's nurse. We are now plunged into the realities of the life of a relatively junior doctor.

We find a flat on the first floor of a fairly large detached house in Wigston Fields, about five miles outside Leicester. Our landlord, Mr Hubbard, is a conjurer and spiritual healer and Mrs Hubbard, a dear old lady (though probably no more than 60!), becomes a close friend and confidante and is constantly worried about the hours that David is working. The Hubbards have séances in their sitting room every Wednesday night and some truly amazing things take place there! The house stands in a wooded area with about an acre of garden surrounding it. We fall in love with it at once and it feels like a princely residence after our small flat in All Farthing Lane.

The pleasure of having what feels like our own proper home soon wanes, however, when David's work schedule kicks in. At first he is very happy to be back at the coalface, but the work schedule is killing; a hundred to a hundred and ten hours a week, a half-day on Saturday and the whole of Sunday off every fortnight. Many a time he is operating for most of the night and then continues to have a full working day. Such hours are no longer permitted by European law but it is from the number of hours of 'cutting' that a junior surgeon like David learns his trade.

I find the loss of David's company devastating at first. He leaves the house at 7.30 am and I am left with the prospect of a whole day on my own, with no assurance that David will even be home for supper. However, it is easier for me to accept these long hours than it would be had I not experienced the medical world myself. I remember acting as the night nurse in charge on the surgical ward, Clayton, when the young surgeon who had come in at 7.30 am to check on his patients, is the same person who is still around at 3.00 am the following morning.

The winter that follows our arrival in Leicester is the coldest since 1947. Snow comes early and remains until spring. It lies so deep in the fields that it is no longer possible to see where the fences are. I somehow manage to keep travelling to London, though train services are uncertain. David never fails to get to the hospital. But the cold is intense and we struggle to keep warm.

I have a memory of the following spring: the snow has melted and Easter has arrived. David has a day off and we decide to go to a hillside near to Loughborough where we know there are badgers. We lie in wait, dressed in army camouflage, careful to be downwind of the badgers. The light is fading; it is just before dusk when we see the first badger emerge and sniff the air. She is followed by three cubs that begin to race around in circles, chasing each other and tumbling down the hillside, totally unaware of us. It is a beautiful sight. We watch for about an hour, until the evening air becomes chilly and the first stars appear. Then we return once more to our warm fireside. Such an event, having time together to 'play' like those young badgers, is so very rare and it has become an extraordinarily vivid memory. It is as though the pleasure of being together has acquired an added intensity because of its rarity.

It is just the same for our friends and colleagues all of whom are, inevitably, in the medical world because they are the only people we meet. A combination of the stress of the job, the lack of home life and the constant moving means many marriages are under great strain. I am lucky to be fully occupied in my own world of music and to have two nights every week with my mother at Reed House. Although it does feel hard, we know this time will pass and things can only get better.

Soon after our arrival in Leicester I return to the Guildhall and am away for two nights and three days each week, managing to fit all my studies, lectures and music lessons into three days. It is no problem for David that I am away because he can eat all his meals in hospital. Without my own full-time occupation, I don't think I could have possibly survived those early months. When David is home he is totally exhausted and there is no opportunity for us to spend leisure time together. Even when we climb in to bed, too tired to think at 11.00 pm, he still has to read The Lancet! Our free times together are like stardust, so special and so rare. If we visit friends or have friends to dine, David is always on call. There are many times when he has to leave for hospital and is unlikely to return before the evening is over.

Johnny and his new wife, Ann, are also having teething problems at the beginning of their marriage although their issue is at the opposite end of the spectrum: John's work, in trading Rolls Royces and Bentleys, is from home, so he is never away. At one of our rare meetings, John remarks, 'The reason why David and Din are so happy together is because they never see each other!'

Things do become easier when we make friends with other doctors and their wives. I become a close friend to Anne, wife of James Hadfield who is also working the same crazy hours. Anne and I keep each other company and I often look after her adorable two-year-old twin girls, Esme and Helen. I long to have babies of my own more than anything in the world.

In August 1963 we have a three week holiday and return to Otter Lodge. The weather is wonderful and after a week of doing nothing David begins to recover. We recapture the sense of joy and adventure of our honeymoon and it is here that our first child, Nicola, is conceived.

That autumn I am happy to find I have certain food cravings, which are followed by a period of all-day nausea when all I can manage to eat is Heinz tomato soup. I feel terrible but at the same time am so happy to think that a baby is at last on the way. When I am next in Byfleet for my weekly visit to my Mum, I have an appointment with her doctor, a newly qualified G.P., who has recently completed a course in midwifery. After examining me he pronounces that there is no pregnancy and that I am suffering a pseudocyesis. I am, of course, totally devastated. He does, however, take a sample of my urine and when this comes back later in the week, it confirms that I am indeed pregnant. However, during the few days of uncertainty I undergo something of the devastation that must be experienced by every woman who longs to conceive and is unable to do so. The disappointment is catastrophic and it feels as though what one has longed for, above everything, all through life, is beyond reach.

The sickness passes after the first three months, but during the period of uncertainty at the beginning, I walk alone across a meadow near to our home and say out loud, 'If I should find a four-leafed clover before I reach the other side of this field that means I *am* pregnant.' I manage to find two! I wonder if this means I am having twins or is it just a resounding affirmation that a baby is on the way! The following day the confirmation arrives.

* * *

By the time Nicola is due David has finished his surgical post in Leicester and is now the senior registrar at Hydestyle, the country branch of St Thomas', near Hazelmere, in Surrey.

We have rented three rooms in a large country house in Chiddingfold, called Combe Court, which is a splendid 18th century mansion with extensive grounds and a lake surrounded by woodland and a bank of rhododendrons and azaleas along its southern border. We have the large original kitchen belonging to the house with a solid fuel Aga, a large bedroom and an adjoining sitting room. Our bedroom overlooks the lawns that lead down to the lake. It feels to us like paradise.

The pace of life is more gentle, and although David is ostensibly resident and is often on call at night and at weekends, the number of calls is relatively few. Our landlady, Miss Fanshawe, is interested in our St Thomas' connection because she had inherited the money she used to buy Combe Court from her aunt who was Florence Nightingale's sister, Parthenon. As a result she gives us rather special treatment.

I continue to attend my lessons and lectures at the Guildhall. When I am nearly nine months pregnant I have my first recital there, which is a big event and part of the final qualification. It is also testing because all my teachers and colleagues will be there, including, of course, Walther Grüner. Never in my life will I have to perform in front of such a knowledgeable, and also critical, audience. However, pregnancy has an extraordinarily calming effect: there is a certain cow-like passivity and an acceptance of how things are without the normal tendency for self-criticism. It is this very quality that is needed for singing because any tension or anxiety affects the breathing and also the body. As one's body is the instrument, any physical tension is bound to affect it adversely. The recital is well received and I pass with flying colours, although there are some ribald remarks about my programme choice: Schubert's *Die Junge Nonne,* sung by a girl with such an obviously big belly!

It is the end of the Easter term and I am nearing the completion of my three years at the Guildhall. I am now free to spend my days exploring the lovely countryside around our home. I walk along the riverbank with a pair of binoculars and I am learning to identify the songs of the birds: different warblers, a blackcap, chiffchaff and, in the evenings, the nightingales. I also observe which trees come first into leaf and learn to recognize different species: the alders along the banks of the stream, the black buds of the ash trees with the flowers which appear before the leaves and the leaves of the ash and black poplars that are the last to appear.

I notice that the leaves on the beech trees outside our bedroom window have turned a lovely new shade of green when I feel my first contractions. It is early May. David is working and has already been told by the obstetrician that he will not be welcome at the birth. The doctor's comment when David asks if he can attend is, 'Would you want me to be there when you are doing a hysterectomy on my wife?' In reality, David wasn't able to be present because he was in the middle of an operating list.

I ring my mother who comes over as quickly as she can, so she is there with me when the contractions become strong and regular. Soon after she arrives we call the ambulance. I am taken straight to a single room in the maternity ward. My mother, who is much more anxious than I am, is told she cannot stay, although to have had her with me would have been a great comfort.

Behind a curtain in the next cubicle is a friend of mine from Thomas', called Helen Hornet. She has just given birth to her daughter and as my contractions become stronger and more regular she gives me words of encouragement, 'It's fine Diana, just breathe deeply, relax as much as you can, don't push yet, it will soon be over and then you will be so happy.'

No nurse comes near me and I am left without support until I can feel the baby arriving. I am rushed into the delivery room and within minutes, the baby arrives.

What a moment that is, when this beautiful little girl is placed in my arms. She is perfect in every way, with her exquisite features, tiny hands and feet and adorable little nose. She already has quite a head of very fine hair. Suddenly, all the stress and pain of the last few hours is forgotten in the overwhelming sense of joy and wonder at this beautiful new life. It is so hard to believe with the first baby that the bump one is carrying can really be a 'live' human being, with an innate nature and potential that will develop, (in so many ways), entirely independently of me.

During my six months working in the midwifery ward at STH I witnessed how the babies were separated from their mothers immediately after birth and not put to the breast for 48 hours, when the milk began to come in. It was maintained that the baby gained nothing by taking in the colostrum.

As a result, the natural instinct of the new-born to latch on and suck was no longer there. As nurses, we then had to spend hours with the mothers teaching the babies to suck. So I ask the nurse to give me my baby daughter the moment she is born, before she is washed and even before the placenta arrives. The midwife is reluctant, saying that no one has ever asked for anything so bizarre before. But the result is that the baby begins to suck straight away and the mother-baby bonding is immediate. I believe that now this is normal practice and that it helps to maintain the contractions for the expulsion of the placenta.

David arrives soon after the birth and is totally delighted with his little daughter. As a present, and to congratulate me on the birth, he brings me a beautiful pair of binoculars, (a very fitting present for the baby who was later to become an ornithologist!).

The baby is taken away from me that night. I am unable to sleep a wink, wondering which of the crying babies is mine. Ostensibly, it is to give the new mothers a good night's sleep but I want my baby beside me, where I can see her, smell her and hear her breathing. So the next morning I discharge myself and my darling mother, who is totally over the moon and delighted with her first grandchild, comes with me. She stays with us at Combe Court for the first fortnight and helps me with breast-feeding and general management, and also makes sure that I rest and can spend two uninterrupted weeks getting to know my baby. She is like a tigress keeping the world at bay so that I can have two weeks of complete rest. It is a really wonderful time for me and David is there whenever he can be. My mother is also a huge practical help to me, not only because she has had three children herself, but also because she is a Truby King trained maternity nurse. My mother-in-law is also trained as a maternity nurse, so I have a wealth of the very best advice!

It is a beautiful summer and I am supremely content with my little daughter. She feeds and sleeps well and we are seldom woken in the night once feeding is well and truly established. David is no longer working all hours so he too has time to enjoy his beautiful daughter. My mother often comes for the day and John makes frequent, unexpected visits. He belongs to a flying club so when I hear the engine of a Tiger Moth and see it zooming low over one of the tall chimneys of Combe Court, I know he is on his way. He is able to land in a nearby field and usually times his visit to coincide with lunch. I spend lazy afternoons lying with my baby beside the lake, watching the iridescent dragonflies as they skim low over the water to land on a lily pad.

At first, I find it hard to believe that this new life is robust enough to survive. Every half hour I check that she is still breathing in her cradle or pram. To me, her aliveness is a total miracle and I think this is true for Mum also. Having lost her eldest son, her belief in life has been affected and she has been in something akin to a depression ever since. Nicola seems to bring her a new connection to life itself so it is a time of great fulfilment for her as well. Nicola is a very special grandchild for the Crockfords also as she is the first of their grandchildren to live in the U.K. They also are frequent visitors that summer and we love to spend weekends at the Oast House when possible.

At the start of the autumn term I return to the Guildhall to complete my studies. Sometimes Nicola comes with me and is looked after by one of Walther's students, while I have my lesson. Otherwise, I leave her with my mother in West Byfleet. I tell Mum what train I will be on, she comes to West Byfleet station and I hand her the baby in her Moses basket and continue to Waterloo on the train. A strong attachment has already developed between little Nicola and my mother.

On the days when I have no classes to attend, I practise at home while Nicola is sleeping in her pram. This arrangement seems to work well for us all and I manage to complete my studies and leave the Guildhall with two diplomas: one for teaching and the other for performing. I am beginning to secure more work in London so Mum comes to look after Nicola during the concerts. One evening I am singing in Haydn's Nelson Mass in Southwark Cathedral. I breastfeed Nicola in the interval; all seems well until the second half when she begins to cry. Mum has to whisk her out. It is the last time we attempt to bring her to a concert.

David completes his one year resident job at Hydestyle and finds himself back again in STH, as a senior registrar. It is a great honour to be employed in his original teaching hospital in a senior post because only the most promising doctors find employment in the hospital where they have trained. Life becomes a little more stressful as he has to catch a 7.00 am train from Witley Station to Waterloo and seldom returns home before 9.00 pm. I find myself envying the other wives whose husbands return home at 6.00 pm and enjoy watching the telly together every evening. But I have my enchanting baby girl who is now walking and chattering and beguiling everyone with her bonny face, her golden curls and rosy cheeks. In my eyes, there has never been a baby as beautiful since the world began!

My mother agrees with me and has written to a friend, an old flame of hers in America, to tell him of her joy in this first grandchild (no doubt she encloses a photo of Nicola). His somewhat sardonic reply is, 'I'm so glad to hear you are delighted with your first grandchild. No doubt the Australians were also pleased when they first saw a rabbit.' I think by that time Michael and Cat Huber had about 30 grandchildren!

We share a joint birthday party for Nicola's first birthday with my friend Helen Hornet and her little girl, Karen, who was, of course, born on the same day. We host it in our big kitchen, with the Aga providing welcome warmth on what is an unseasonably chilly day.

Soon after this we once again holiday at Otter Lodge. Nicola enjoys being with both her parents for 24 hours a day and for David and me it is a time to recapture once more the joy of being at leisure; now we are together as a family and have days of uninterrupted time that have been so very rare. It is here that once again a baby is conceived.

Nicola with David

Nicola with my Mum

Nicola with her Mum

Chapter 11

Family Life

Your children are not your children.
They are the sons and daughters of life's longing for itself.
They come through you but not from you,
And though they are with you, yet they belong not to you....

You are the bows from which your children as living arrows are sent forth

(Khalil Gibran: The Prophet).

David is soon to become a consultant general surgeon at St Thomas', but he quite suddenly decides that he no longer wants to be a general surgeon. He is increasingly discouraged by the continual stress and the long hours that are involved. The pressure of the waiting lists as well as the unhelpful attitude of the labour government with Barbara Castle as the unsympathetic Minister of Health, has been creating increasing antagonism within the medical profession.

He makes the decision to transfer to plastic surgery, which at first means a considerable loss of both status and salary. He is accepted in a junior post at Frenchay Hospital in Bristol and finds himself once again a senior house surgeon. There is a senior registrar post imminent, which he is hoping to apply for. So, once again we are on the move. Andrew Henderson introduces us to a friend of his called Angela Shepherd, who is a junior doctor working in Bristol. She is living at her parents' home in Tockington, near Bristol, and invites us to stay with her until we can rent somewhere not too far from Frenchay Hospital.

It isn't an easy time for any of us. Nicola is unsettled by the move and I have severe morning sickness. David is trying to grasp an entirely unfamiliar branch of surgery in a new environment as well as finding us somewhere to live. Not only do I have no car to go house-hunting, but I am also feeling unwell for the whole day and am, for a time, unable to keep any food down. Angela is a great help and support to us and becomes a close friend, seeing us through a very tricky patch. Later we invite her to be Helena's godmother. My mother comes to stay and help whenever she is able. Nicola, from having been a secure and independent eighteen month-old toddler, becomes so insecure I can't even spend a penny without her being with me.

She is just beginning to say her first words; after Mummy and Daddy the first word she learns is Emma, the name of the Shepherds' beautiful golden labrador. When my Mum comes to stay she isn't yet able to say 'Grandma' but she can manage 'Ama', which is very close to the sound of 'Emma'. So, my Mum becomes known as 'Annema', and this is how she is later to be known by all her grandchildren.

Finally, we find the charming Old School House, in Aust. It is the first time we have had an entire house to ourselves and once again, it feels a little like a children's game of playing at Mummys and Daddys as we spread our few belongings around an entire house with two bedrooms and a study as well as a sitting room. It seems palatial! The house has its own garden and is only a few hundred yards from the ferry, which crosses the Severn Estuary to Chepstow. The construction of the Severn Bridge, which at the time was supposed to be the longest bridge in England, is not completed until after we leave the area. So, when I go to Cardiff for my weekly singing lessons I need to take the ferry.

This singing teacher is a whole new kettle of fish and so very different from Walther Grüner. She is large, ebullient and as warmly appreciative with her praise as Walther was cautious. I flourish under her enthusiasm and warmth. In her strong Austrian accent she tells me, 'If you do not continue to sing it will be a sin against God as well as yourself.' Well, how could I think of stopping after such affirmation? It almost seemed as if the oracle had spoken! She had been a magnificent Isolde in her youth, but after a thyroid operation she says she can now only sing bass.

It is early April and our second baby is due. One day I am walking in our village, pushing Nicola in the pram, when suddenly I am aware of a deluge of liquid and realize that my waters have broken. I manage to get home intact; soon afterwards David returns from the hospital. We ring the midwife who asks us to let her know when the contractions become more frequent. We are allowed to have the baby at home this time.

I make supper and put Nicola to bed. Then we wait. It is probably about 10.00 pm when we finally ring our attractive young midwife, who arrives in approximately ten minutes. When the contractions start to come in earnest, David is beside me, rubbing my back. How different it is from the first time when I had felt totally abandoned. He provides a running commentary of encouraging words; in-between contractions I dance around the room, dressed only in one of David's cast-off shirts. The midwife is urging me to jump up and down to hasten the baby's arrival. So I dance and David and the nurse cheer me on. Just before midnight on the 4th of April, on the eve of the new financial year, (which from a tax point of view seemed to be very important), our little daughter is born. She is petite and totally beautiful with large, wide-open eyes from the very moment of her birth. I hold her and she goes immediately to the breast and once again the joy and wonder I experience with the arrival of this perfect baby surpasses everything.

At seven the next morning Nicola comes into our room. We have bought her a doll and the blind man who made our bamboo cradle for Nicola has made us a doll's size cradle to match, which we have placed beside the baby's cradle in which Helena is now peacefully sleeping. Nicola comes into our room, goes straight over to the baby's cradle, totally ignoring the doll, and has a quick peek inside. She sees the sleeping baby and then goes over to my dressing table where she examines herself in the mirror. I see her face in the reflection, registering that some traumatic and life-changing event has occurred. We try to interest her in the doll but to no avail, as though she already recognizes that this is just a diversionary ploy. I give her a cuddle, but she already seems to know that the world, which so far has belonged entirely to her, will have to be shared from now on and that her place in the scheme of things will never be quite the same again.

Is there anything that one can do to alleviate the shock and total loss that the first child experiences when a second baby arrives; when she or he is no longer the whole focus of attention and centre of the world? Someone once said, 'It's all very well to say, 'Mummy and Daddy love you just as much as before.' How would it feel if the husband brought a new woman into the house and said to his wife, 'I love you just as much as I did before?' Most people, unless brought up as a Muslim, wouldn't buy it! The whole business of sharing proves to be difficult for Nicola and as Helena grows and demands more attention it doesn't become any easier.

Helena is an exceptionally beautiful and contented baby with unusually big wide-awake eyes and a solemn face. She almost never cries, as though even at this stage she can feel that there isn't enough attention to go around. She has a tiny bleat of a cry; I often can't tell the difference between her crying and the bleating of the new lambs in the nearby fields. She feeds lustily and begins to sleep through the night by the time she is two months old. As she grows older she becomes totally fascinated by Nicola. Regardless of what else is going on, she never takes her eyes off her big sister, who can make her laugh and chuckle in a way that no one else can.

When Helena is four months old, David applies for a job in Newcastle, having failed to secure the senior post in plastic surgery in Bristol. Newcastle seems to us an impossibly distant and dark place; we only associate it with industry, poverty and coal. However, when he successfully secures the job we have no alternative but to move, yet again. It is a big disruption because by this time we feel well settled in Aust. David enjoys the unit and companionship at Frenchay Hospital and we have made many friends.

Nicola is also settled in the little nursery school I have started with my friend, Hilary Holden. We take it in turns to have six children in our homes, although Hilary's home is preferable because they have a large garden, swings and slides, dogs and cats and, best of all, a donkey. Nicola is happy with this family and has fallen head over heels in love with their four year old son, Daniel. She is happy also to be left with Hilary when I go for my weekly lessons to Cardiff. After a year in Aust we have begun to believe this to be our permanent home. I have even created a vegetable garden and grow enough to supply our needs.

It is true that David is once again working very long hours, but we have somehow come to expect this. However, one day we realize the impact of this on the children when David, unusually, is at home for Sunday lunch. Nicola, now three years old, comments, 'What are you doing at home Daddy, why aren't you at the hospital?' David's involvement with the children at this stage in their lives is minimal and is really restricted to our annual summer holiday. This isn't something that is an issue for us, because it is simply what we know and expect as part of medical life. But the absence of a Dad *is* hard for his children

Johnny and Christopher

It isn't possible for David to take time off work to house-hunt in Newcastle. However, my half brother, Christopher, just happens to be in the UK at the time, having come over from New Zealand with the idea of possibly returning to the U.K. with his family of eight children. He is thinking about buying a farm somewhere and Northumberland is one of the places that he believes could offer what he is looking for, so he and my mother set off by car to look at a possible house for us to rent, not too far from the city.

They find a 1930s semi in Ponteland in a road called Cheviot View; on a fine day, it is indeed possible to get a view of Cheviot's distant peak. The house has a small garden and a patch in front with enough room to park a car. This road is an established area; many of our neighbours have lived here their entire lives and are now in their '60s and '70s. Apart from one other medical couple, Tina and Bill Ryder, who are both anaesthetists, we are the only young family in Cheviot View.

David commutes the six miles into the Royal Victoria Infirmary and starts again as a middle grade registrar, this time as a plastic surgeon. Our misgivings about the north-east are unfounded. We receive a warm welcome and I soon make friends with other young mums. The first person I befriend is Margaret Dobson, whom I meet at the doctor's surgery during a clinic for young Mums. Margaret asks me about my two daughters. I tell her their ages - two and a half and six months - so a good two years between them. Margaret's daughters are less than a year apart in age and her wry comment to me is, '*You* must have heard about birth control!' We both laugh and take an immediate liking to one another.

Margaret calls unexpectedly the following day. I have just been on my knees scrubbing the kitchen floor and am now perched on the edge of the kitchen table drinking a cup of coffee with a duster tied around my head. Helena is asleep in her pram and Nicola is playing with her toys on the kitchen floor. I feel that a visitor could never have seen me at a greater disadvantage! Margaret walks straight in, joins me with a cup of coffee and makes an instant rapport with Nicola. We sit and talk like old friends and I know at once that we will get on together.

This occasion must be just a few days before Christmas because she invites us all over for drinks on Boxing Day. I tell her that my parents-in-law will be with us and without hesitation, she includes them as well. I telephone the Dobsons later to confirm and to find out directions to their house. Margaret's husband, Norman, answers. I tell him about Margaret's invitation; his response is, 'Oh my God!' We soon discover that this is a typical Norman response. In the end, however, we are unwell and unable to go. An important friendship has nevertheless begun, and for many years Margaret is my closest friend, until her sad and premature death just before her 60th birthday. Our lives would interweave in many ways and it is as a result of an introduction from Margaret and Norman that I would meet my second husband Chris, after David's death. But this is still a long way ahead!

Our other friends at this time are Bill and Tina Ryder.

One day I have a visit from Tina who has just landed a part-time job in anaesthetics at the Royal Victoria Infirmary in Newcastle and has no babysitter. She wonders if she can employ me to take care of her little girl, Karen, who is just a few months younger than Nicola. I am delighted to have a companion for Nicola and soon form a strong attachment to Karen. She is big for her age, very advanced and like Nicola, has a head of golden curls. When I take the two for walks along the pavement of our busy road, together with Helena in her pram, many a mum stops me, thinking the two girls are twins. Having Karen is also helpful for Nicola and gives her an opportunity to play with a child of her own age; to share her toys and also her mum!

Tina only works in the mornings but sometimes, if a list is delayed, she arrives home well after lunch. However, Karen, who is always happy to be with us, refuses to eat anything. She knows her mother will be home to give her lunch and it is almost as though she fears that if she has her lunch with us her mother won't come home.

We leave our Cheviot View house by the following autumn and as we are now secure in the knowledge that David will eventually be appointed to the senior registrar post in Newcastle, we decide to buy a small semi in a new housing estate, for the colossal sum of £4,400.00. We have the best house in the road: the one belonging to the Barratt builder responsible for the estate's construction. The house is less than five years old and is therefore in perfect condition. However, it has a stuffy smell we are unable to get rid of, especially in our bedroom, so before we move in we rip up all the fitted carpets and sand the pine floors.

Until now we have only rented furnished houses, so we possess no furniture. Our first two pieces are an antique oak press and the lower part of an oak antique dresser, which we think are beautiful. We pay £25 for each in the Corbridge antique shop. Soon we have gathered beds, kitchen furniture and some old pine wardrobes. It is an amazing feeling to have a home that really belongs to us, especially as we have already had so many temporary, rented homes. We are also the owners of at least 20 x 30 yards of Northumberland, which is the sum total of our back garden and tiny front garden. No home has ever felt so complete and satisfactory! However, we are told that we are only the owners of the land itself; what lies above and below the land belongs to the state, i.e. if we were suddenly to find a source of coal or oil when digging our cabbage patch! Fortunately, no hidden seams of coal come to light!

The children soon make friends with other young children and our house is often filled with half the children who live in the road. Nicola begins to attend a nursery school in Darras Hall, a one mile walk away, and I am now pregnant with our third baby. Our mode of transport is a large carriage pram, which is big enough to hold two children and our shopping. There is a convenient row of shops at the end of Thornhill Road, so I can gather any necessary supplies on our way back from delivering Nicola to nursery school. Without a car our range of activities is limited but there is a park on the way to Nicola's nursery with a river running through it and the mums often meet there with their toddlers.

Our new baby is due on my birthday, June 5th, but she is one day late and arrives on June 6th. Once again, my Mum comes to stay and this time attends the birth. There is some pressure from the family for me to have a son; David is the last in the Crockford family's male line. My mother-in-law especially has made it clear that I must produce a son. The night before Catherine is born I dream that I have a little daughter and my brother, Johnny, says to me in the dream, 'Don't worry Din, plastic surgery is now so advanced it is possible to make a girl baby into a boy.' I cry, 'No, no, no, I want my little daughter just the way she is.' So, when she arrives the following day my beautiful daughter is the most wonderful birthday gift I have ever had!

My friend Gale Middleton, who lives with her husband Miles and their two children, Georgina and Nicholas, has taken Nicola and Helena for a walk until the birth is over. It occurs very swiftly at 3.00 pm; by the time David arrives it is over. When the baby is bathed and in her crib the children return and rush up to see their new sister. Nicola takes one look at the small red face and tiny form wrapped in her shawl and shouts, 'Hurray, it's a girl, I won't have to throw it out of the window.' It's a mystery how she knew the sex of the baby because noone had told her!

Lying with my baby for ten days following the birth, while my mother looks after the rest of the household is a time of rest and of pure joy as I have time to get to know my new daughter. I hear the commotion downstairs as Annema attempts to protect me from too many visitors and the needs and squabbles of two children. I think, 'This baby will be a peace maker, she will bring joy where ever she goes.' How prophetic this has proved to be!

The months following Cathy's birth are perhaps the most exhausting and unrelenting of my whole life. I remember thinking how easy it must have been in my early nursing days at St Thomas' when we had three hours off a day! As a young Mum without help and with three children of four and under, there is no time off until we sink exhausted into bed.

After Cathy's birth we buy our first washing machine and soon afterwards my lovely mother-in-law pays for me to have a morning's help each week, which is when Mrs Stevenson (always known as Stevie) comes into our lives. She comes on a Wednesday when the house is normally in a state of chaos, with children fighting and screaming and Diana at her wits end. When she arrives peace is suddenly restored, the children cluster around her and she leaves the house shining from top to bottom. She has a wonderful quality and a calm and gentle nature which is like balm for us all; the children adore her and she remains with us for many years. For me she is a life-saver and I feel restored after her weekly visit! She also baby-sits for us; as the children grow older she plays whist with them and they gamble for sweets. Baby-sitting nights are popular, especially as in those early days I am very strict about sweets and they are normally severely restricted!

We are all young mums in these new houses and we help one another. There are three families in particular whose children are the same ages as ours: the Middletons, the Rutherfords and the Hodgesons. The children play in each other's houses and the road is quiet enough for them to go safely from house to house. When there is a difficulty the mums help each other out. On one occasion I have a nasty bout of 'flu and my curtains are still drawn at 9.00 am. It isn't long before the front door bell is ringing - ding dong, ding dong - and Shirley is at the door, calling up the stairs, 'Diana, can I do anything for you? The shopping, or take the children?' Help is always at hand. It is an amazingly supportive place for a young mum who cannot expect her overworked husband to be around in any domestic sense.

Gale was the person, from this time, who was to become a life-long friend. We have supported one another through life's ups and downs and have shared many lovely holidays together. She has been a part of all our family celebrations over the years; marriages, funerals and important birthdays. As one grows older, these life long friendships seem to grow in importance.

When Cathy is a few months old I begin to sing again and find myself increasingly in demand as a soloist with choirs in and around Newcastle, mainly (at this stage) as an oratorio singer. If David is not around Stevie comes to look after the children; concerts are generally held in the evenings, when the children are safely asleep. I particularly remember, shortly before Cathy's birth, singing the alto solos in a performance of the St. John Passion for John Healy in the church of St James and St Basil in Heaton. The famous tenor who is singing the Evangelist role for the 113th time seems almost as nervous as I am. A few weeks later he is talking to a friend of mine who asks if he remembers singing recently with Diana Crockford. He replies that he has a clear image of a very 'fecund figure who was reading a book entitled 'Love Is Not Enough'' (by Bruno Bettelheim). What he thought of her singing is not recorded!

Helena and Cathy

Chapter 12

America

The Land of the Free and the home of the brave.
(Francis Scott Key).

When Cathy is just two years old David has an opportunity to move to New York for a year to work with American plastic surgeons. Anyone interested in cosmetic surgery needed to do time in the US. It is known among plastic surgeons as a mandatory part of their training...their BTA (or, Been To America).

A friend of ours who has recently separated from her husband is looking for a place to rent for a year. So, for a modest rent, Alison Striciavic, as she was then, (later, after her marriage to Anthony, to become Alison Brown), comes to live in our little house in Ponteland and looks after the house and our cat, Moppet, for a year. We set sail with our three little girls, minimum possessions and considerable excitement, to a very different life in New York City.

We board Queen Elizabeth II and are seen off by our dear friend, Andrew Henderson and his new young wife, Non. She is still in her bohemian phase and the children are fascinated to see her climb on board with bare feet. Little did we know at the time how close Andrew was to come to dying of cancer while we were away. He was diagnosed with an aggressive cancer of the bladder just two months after their wedding and was given six months to live. It was Non, with her determination and dedication, who saved his life and gave him once again the will to live after a year of unremitting pain and suffering. We had letters from Andrew while we were away, but we didn't realise until our return home what a close call it had been.

For a week on the QEII we live in the lap of luxury.

There is a crèche for the children and every kind of amusement is available. Being waited on at table is a new experience and being allowed an unlimited supply of ice cream at every meal is a delight never to be repeated! The children are not happy to be left in the crèche so that is of little use. Cathy, aged two, is too young to be left unattended for a moment because it is quite possible to find a way through the protective barrier. She could so easily slip over board, so we have to attach reins to her at all times.

From the dock in New York we take a taxi out to Riverdale and the small gatehouse that is to be our home for the next year. Once again, it is my mother's friend, Barbara Bosanquet, who has arranged this for us. Her daughter, Kirsty, has been living at the Dodge Estate with her young family throughout the previous year; they are about to leave New York and the house is now vacant. The Dodge family are her distant cousins and they are very happy to welcome us to their estate for what is a peppercorn rent of just $45 a month. Polly Dodge writes David a welcoming letter detailing the rent and asking if it is too much. David thinks we could afford this on his tiny salary. We later discover that the going rate for accommodation in a far less salubrious part of NY would be in the region of $150 a month!

Our taxi brings us to 4695, Independence Avenue where we find a tiny, grey-slated gatehouse cottage set in parkland of 35 acres. This is to be our home for the next year. We are totally unprepared for such an astonishingly beautiful place: acres of mown grass and mature trees set alongside the Hudson River. We have the use of a playground for the children and a fine swimming pool. We feel as if we have arrived in heaven and the children suddenly have a freedom and the potential for expansive exploration, which has never been possible in our tiny garden in Northumberland.

Polly and Cleve Dodge live in a fine stone house

overlooking the river; there are five or six other houses belonging to their children or other relatives, scattered across the parkland. We have the freedom to roam over the whole area. With typical American hospitality, Polly Dodge soon introduces us to all our neighbours within the Dodge Estate and everyone provides items of furniture, so we are soon fully furnished. We are able to spend the first few weeks in an apartment above the Dodge family's garage while our house is being equipped with essentials. We arrive to a fridge that has been filled with food and we soon feel happily at home.

David has few clinical responsibilities to begin with so we are to see more of him than ever before. It is a change for us all to have a husband and dad who isn't permanently tired. We arrive in Riverdale in early June when the gardens are still full of colour and flowers are in full bloom. It is sunny but not too hot and the children are able to play naked on the small lawn outside our house.

But after two weeks, the heat of a New York summer takes over. We are totally unprepared for it; it isn't just the temperature, which was in the 30's, centigrade but the heat combined with the humidity. But by this time we have become members of the estate swimming pool, of which we have unlimited use. We head there at the beginning of the day, when the intense heat builds, and remain beside the water until dusk. I am completely felled by the heat - an enervating heat such as I have never experienced before. I am unable, for a time, to fulfil any household chores; our house, with no air-conditioning, is like a furnace. I dream of the leafy lanes of Northumberland cooled with a fresh sea breeze. Nicola would come down from her bedroom in the evening, unable to sleep due to the closeness and the heat. I remember her coming to us in tears; she had been trying to sleep naked, on the bare boards of her bedroom floor. She wails, 'I just need to take off my skin.' For a time, I feel I will never survive; every day the radio weather reports provide an air pollution reading, which can be as high as 100%. I begin to understand why anyone who can afford to moves away from New York during the summer months.

The houses around us are mostly empty that first summer so we don't meet many of our neighbours until the fall. We do soon acclimatise to the New York climate and before long feel a part of this young and vibrant community. There are two families in particular whose children become almost a part of our family: the Betts and the Macks. The Macks live down the road and are separate from the Dodge Estate. They have a daughter, Lorna, of Helena's age, so we often exchange daughters. Helena spends much of her time that summer playing at the Macks' house. One day, Cathy is missing. I discover her half way down the road on a tiny tricycle, on her way to visit the Mack family. Fortunately, it is a very quiet road. Helena is able to walk there on her own, which gives her a little respite from her increasingly bossy older sister!

Glynne Betts is a divorcee with three children; their youngest daughter, Kate, spends more time at our house than in her own. It seems at first strange to me that she seems to prefer our home - where the children have scarcely any toys or possessions - to her own. But I soon realize that with a mum who is working as a photographer and an absent dad, she is just enjoying a normal family life. Their son, Will, is 10 years old and bordering on delinquency, having set fire to various places. We are the only family who still welcome him, so he also becomes a regular visitor to our home. On one of our visits to the NY zoo he comes with us and sits next to Helena in the car. On the way he proposes to her. Helena refuses him, and Cathy, aged two and a half, not wanting his feelings to be hurt says, 'Don't worry, I'll marry you Will'.

Our children are also welcome visitors at the Betts' house. Sometimes I find that Cathy is no longer in her cot when I go to wake her early in the morning. She has simply disappeared over to the Betts for breakfast, still in her wet nappy from the night! Nicola also loves to visit the family and has a particular passion for Glynne, a beautiful young woman who Nicola christens, 'Princess'. This is the name by which she becomes known. When Nicola returns from school every day, she runs down the lane from the school bus, throws her school satchel into our little garden and runs straight on to visit Princess. Glynne becomes the princess from Sleeping Beauty, or from Snow White, while I am always the Wicked Witch. Nicola would say, 'Today I saw Princess working in the garden,' and I might reply, 'Well, so what, I too have been working in the garden.' 'Ah yes,' says Nicola, 'But *she* is a princess and princesses don't work.' The implication is, I think, that for a commoner like me, work is what you *do.*

We have a lovely neighbour, known to everyone as Mrs B. She is married to the estate gardener and is a universal nanny to all the children on the estate. She has an understanding of children and a wisdom that comes from enormous experience of overly-indulged, and at the same time emotionally deprived, rich, American children. Nicola adores her. When David and I go away for three days to San Francisco for a Plastic Surgery conference, Mrs B comes to look after the children. It is the first time I have left them. Before we leave, Mrs B says, 'While you're away, I will become the *bad* one and you will become the *Princess.* And so it was!

The days in San Francisco are unforgettable. It is the first time that David and I have been alone since the advent of children. That is a wonderful experience in itself. But the beauty and magic of San Francisco bowls us over, with its cobbled streets and views of the sea when the trams reach the high point of the steeply-rising inclines, and we catch a sudden glimpse of the Golden Gate Bridge gleaming in the sun. The atmosphere is cosmopolitan, with a large Chinese and European population, while Americans here are at their most open-hearted and unprejudiced. Even in the 1960s it isn't unusual to see two gay men walking together in the street, hand in hand.

The magic may in part be due to the amazing feeling of being unencumbered by children. Every time I hear a child calling, 'Mummy', I instinctively look around, expecting to be needed by someone. But it is also the joy of being together and being *alone* together, for the first time in six years. It is a little like falling in love all over again!

Flying from NY to San Francisco is further than flying from NY to the UK, but although we only have three days in the city it is certainly worth it. For us it has been an unforgettable time! I remember saying that if we were to live in the USA permanently - this possibility did in fact arise - I would be very happy to settle in San Francisco, but New York would definitely be out of the question. One of the particularly attractive aspects of San Francisco is the climate, which is generally sunny but never too hot and never too cold. The pace of life is gentler, and more European.

During our time in San Francisco David and I were able to visit my father's old friend and colleague, Joseph Henderson. He was the father of Jungian psychology on the West Coast, together with his close friend, Joseph Wheelwright. We stayed the night in their beautiful home in Sausalito, in Marin County, just across the Golden Gate Bridge from San Francisco. I had always heard so much about Joe from my mother and I was especially delighted to meet his wife, Helena, who was the eldest child of the friend of my childhood, Frances Cornford. Joe was later to become an important source of information for me when I embarked on the writing of my father's biography – as the only person still living who had known him, (with the exception of my father's second daughter, Chloe, who lived to be 99 years old). We were warmly welcomed by both Helena and Joe and it was, indeed, a memorable visit.

Nicola, Helena and Cathy

We make many friends in New York, both with the friends and family members of the Dodge Estate and also with David's colleagues. He works in two hospitals, which represent the opposite ends of the U.S. medical spectrum. The first is the New York Medical Centre, one of the most modern and high tech hospitals in the world. It is for private patients only, so it is for the few who can afford the colossal cost of medical insurance. The second hospital is called Belle View, which supplies medical care for those who have no insurance and who cannot afford to pay. Here, the conditions are positively medieval. The same doctors work in both, but the medical provision and equipment at Belle View is minimal and the standard of cleanliness abysmal. Not long before David starts working there, rats are seen scurrying around the beds and pigeons flying about in the wards. It makes us tremendously grateful for the NHS. The standard of medicine among doctors also varies widely. David comes across one doctor who has for years been treating an old woman for Addison's Disease, knowing that in reality there is nothing wrong with her. She is rich and he is pocketing a tidy sum of money. David finds these revelations deeply distressing. But at the time they seem to be endemic in American society.

American hospitality is, however, heart-warming. We have invitations from all members of the Dodge family and from Polly and Cleve in particular. Dinner parties include many interesting people: Cleve's sister, Mrs Clarke, known to us as Auntie, is a friend and frequent visitor to the Secretary General of the United Nations, U Thant. At one time her husband had been the Vice Chancellor of the University of Istanbul; they were living in Turkey when Ataturk made it illegal for a woman to wear the veil in public. The university gave a great reception; only women who were not veiled were allowed to attend. For many of these women it was the first time in their lives that they had appeared in public without the veil, which must have been a daunting experience. Cleve himself, who was, at 80, still commuting to work every day, was a big man in the City. He was the owner of copper mines in Arizona as well as an island in the St Lawrence River. However, the person that David was most interested to meet was the father of plastic surgery in America, Gerry Webster. He was one of the Vanderbilt family, the original owners of Manhatten Island, and was a near neighbour in Riverdale. We developed a warm friendship with him and were often invited to dine at his beautiful home. The children enjoyed his swimming pool, full of exciting inflatable toys; a crocodile, a whale and a dolphin, while David and I were served exotic, alfresco meals by the butler, in the rose arbour nearby.

Dining at the Dodges is a grand affair. We sit at their fine dining table with views of the Hudson River through the picture windows and enjoy delicious meals served to us by their Puerto Rican butler and maid. At other times, Polly invites the children and me to tea. A low table is set for the three children beside the large window from which we can see the river, always crowded with boats and barges, lying far below. Cucumber sandwiches are served on Dresden china plates, tea in elegant china cups and the children are served hot crumpets and cake by the maid in her lacy white apron. I sit beside Polly in anticipation of spills and disaster but somehow the solemnity of the occasion impresses the children and they behave as though we are in church. Polly says she has never before experienced such beautifully behaved children. This subsequently becomes a family joke!

Warm hospitality is also extended to us from David's colleagues. In early May, during our second summer in New York, a fellow senior registrar offers David the loan of his yacht for a week's holiday. We sail down the Hudson River as far as Oxford, Maryland, on Chesapeake Bay. What a wonderful holiday it is, with David again enjoying the delight of skippering a fine yacht and dreaming that he is the owner of this splendid vessel; a dream that was never to become a reality. This is just one of many holidays we had that memorable year.

We spend our first summer with the Osborns in Maine. Fred and Nancy, who have not yet had any grandchildren of their own, are enchanted by our three girls, and treat them like their own family. We sail and swim and take part in the family singsongs and explore the countryside; for me it is like old times again. Once more I am a part of this warm and loving family. David is also accepted as another family member. David, the children and I have a log cabin to ourselves; in the neighbouring cabin is Fred's nephew, John Osborn, and his young wife. At the time John is involved in writing his book, *The Paper Chase,* which would become a best seller and television series and is based on his experiences at Harvard Law School. He does not find the proximity of three noisy children compatible with his writing and is not slow in letting them know how unwelcome they are! They find him a grumpy young man, but it doesn't spoil their enjoyment. I believe when his own children began to arrive he learned to be a little more tolerant!

The person who does win the children's hearts is Charlie, who is now 15 years old. He is tall, gangling, endlessly patient and enjoys nothing more than entertaining three eager little girls. Cathy is inclined to wander off into the meadow of long grass just below the main cabin. She can be found among the wild flowers and her fair hair looks like the downy seed heads of the thistles and dandelions. Nancy christens her 'Thistledown' and this is how she becomes known.

On one occasion, we take the children on a boat trip to Bar Harbour, an hour's voyage across the Bay from Asheville and Tranquility Farm. During the afternoon David and I have a minor altercation. We return to the farm where Nancy asks about our afternoon. Nicola is six and is already in charge of the world. She replies, 'Mummy is thinking of marrying again as she and Daddy can't agree.' We have to reassure Nancy that the split-up isn't imminent!

We take another holiday, camping in Vermont, to enjoy the dazzling spectacle of the Fall colours. We wake early in the morning to a collage of reds, oranges and yellows that stretch in every direction as far as the eye can see. It looks as though the sun is shining, yet there is no sun. It is a sight of stunning beauty. We have no tent, but the children sleep in the back of our VW station wagon and David and I sleep in our sleeping bags inside the small cabin that each campsite provides. The American campsites are well equipped and each camper has their own rather private area, which is supplied with a barbecue and wood and a small covered area, so we are able to see some far-flung areas of the States at a minimal cost. What fun it is!

On another occasion we take cousin Adi with us and camp on the banks of the Shenandoah River in Virginia. It is Easter and the river is high and fast-flowing from the recent snow-melt. We hide Easter eggs for the children in rabbit holes along the banks and in the clefts of tall maple trees. Adi, a confident ten year old, finds most of the eggs so his basket is full, while the girls have found almost none and little Cathy, none at all. So, Adi must reluctantly share his hoard and in the end, everyone is happy.

The following day the sun appears; a hot sun which melts all the remaining snow in a single day. Suddenly it is summer. There is no spring in America, as we know it. We take the children to see the stalactites and stalagmites in the limestone caverns, in the Blue Ridge Mountains of Virginia. It is like going into a cathedral. Some of the stalagmites are like sculptures; one could be the Virgin Mary holding the infant Christ. The piped music adds to the mystical experience. The children are silent and there is a sense of something awesome in that deep underground cavern.

Christmas that year is one that none of us will ever forget. We drive up to Ottawa to stay with David's elder sister, Meg and her Swiss husband, Hans. It is like Christmas from a fairy story. The snow is already nearly three feet deep and we drive north through a snowstorm with the snow blowers clearing the road ahead of us as we drive. As we approach Meg and Hans' Swiss-style chalet near Ottawa, we see that all the houses along the roadside have icicles hanging from their rooves, some as long as 12–18 inches, which shimmer in the Christmas lights. The children are still wide awake as we drive through the night; it is exquisitely beautiful and the way Christmases are supposed to be!

The following morning Christoph, who is just 15 years old, (the eldest of Meg and Hans' three sons), goes out across their farm on his cross-country skis in search of a Christmas tree from the surrounding woodland. He brings one home on his shoulders and we all help with the decorations. It is Christmas Eve and we have the Christmas meal to prepare because, Swiss-style, they celebrate with presents and feasting the night before Christmas. We all help with the meal and by the time it comes to opening presents the three little girls are exhausted. When Meg says, 'You are not able to open a present until you've recited a poem,' Cathy bursts into tears. The other two are beyond even unwrapping their parcels. It is now nearly 1.00 am; they are past caring.

Christmas day dawns bright and fiercely cold: it is 30 degrees below zero (centigrade). The children are excited to venture out into the snow and Meg fits us all out - even two-year-old Cathy - with skis and boots. We head through nearby woods to the local ski trails and are soon proficient enough on our cross-country skis to enjoy racing along the ski trails as though we'd been doing it all our lives. It is an exhilarating feeling and an unforgettable sight as we speed through the forest among snow-covered conifers, along trails of deep snow and with vistas beyond to the Gatineau Hills.

The next day, we are having our breakfast at the long dining room table. Cathy is seated beside me on a couple of cushions so that her head can reach above the table. Suddenly, she lets out a cry of surprise. She is just putting a piece of toast into her mouth when Bert, the tame sparrow, lands on her toast with the idea of sharing it. It is Cathy's first encounter with Bert and she does not yet know him as a friend. The shock and surprise of this encounter remains as her earliest memory; she is just two and a half years old.

We return to Canada the following summer when it is a very different world; the Weber's life now revolving around the farm. There are pigs to feed and a cow to milk and it is hay-making time. We live outside but the plagues of black fly seem to pursue us wherever we go. Little Nicola seems to be particularly succulent and soon her eyelids are so swollen from bites she can scarcely see. The children swim and enjoy being with cousin Adi while Christoph and

Richard are now young men driving the tractor, making hay, and canoeing when help is not needed on the farm.

The whole North American adventure has been an important experience for all of us, but now we are ready to go home.

Chapter 13

Home Again

A dust whom England bore, shaped, made aware,
Gave once her flowers to love, her ways to roam,
A body of England's, breathing English air,
Washed by the rivers, blest by suns of home.
And think this heart, all evil shed away,
A pulse in the eternal mind, no less
Gives somewhere back the thoughts by England given;
Her sights and sounds; dreams happy as her day;
And laughter, learned of friends; and gentleness,
In hearts at peace, under an English heaven.

Rupert Brooke: *The Soldier*

We come home to our little house in Thornhill Road and soon return to the rhythm of our northern lives. Cathy is now three and refers to our old home as 'the New World', and New York becomes 'the Old World', which is the only world she can remember.

Nicola and Helena go to the local primary school in Ponteland. Nicola is now well ahead, having been with children a year older than herself in New York. She is reading the *Narnia* books of C.S. Lewis and identifying with their adventures. Helena has learned to read in New York, partly through my teaching but also through playing 'schools' with Nicola. She is just five years old and can read fluently. But this is not to her advantage when she begins school because the teacher, Mrs Hall, gives all her attention to the children who are learning to read, and Helena is left to read on her own. She is very unhappy; during the first weeks of school she runs home – a five-minute walk away – during the lunch break and I have to return a very reluctant little girl for afternoon school. However, she soon makes a friend and all is well.

There is still no assurance that David will be appointed to a senior post in Plastic Surgery in Newcastle. First, negotiations must begin with the Government to make the case for an extra post in plastic surgery in the north-east. A waiting list of several years leaves no question about the need. However, we have now outgrown our three-bedroom semi and feel it is time to look, after so many moves, for our permanent home. First, we look in Gosforth, (a leafy area of Newcastle), which is close to where the children would later attend a small private school, called Westfield. We have heard that there is an enlightened and outstanding headmistress. She believes in instilling in children a love of learning, in contrast to those schools which force-feed knowledge into their pupils, in order to pass exams.

We visit a house in Montague Avenue, which is just a five-minute walk from the school, and is one of the finest streets in Gosforth. The house has three stories and half an acre of garden, which backs onto the Town Moor: an area of open country in the heart of the city where cows are able to graze. We put in an offer for the asking price and it is accepted. However, the builder J.T.Bell comes to view the house on the same day and gazumps us, saying that he can produce the cash immediately and requires no survey. Our good fairy was certainly looking out for us that day; this turns out to be a stroke of luck. A life growing up within a big city would have been a very different upbringing to the country life that our daughters later experienced.

At the same time, there is another house for sale in a tiny village called Dalton, which lies ten miles to the north west of Newcastle. It is the same price as the first but is no more than a ramshackle cottage in need of a great deal of renovation. We fall in love with this house, the spacious garden and the environs. We had dreamed about our children growing up in this kind of home. Dalton is just three miles from the sophistication of Ponteland and Darras

Hall, but it is like going back 50 years in time.

Apart from the Fenwick family, who live in the Big House, we are the first outsiders in this tiny village of farmers. At first, we are viewed with suspicion and a little hostility until, after some years, David has performed an operation on a member of almost every family in the village. Most of the villagers have lived here all their lives and their parents and grandparents before them. A man called Joe Twizel, who brings us bowls of delicious strawberries from his garden every summer, has never ventured further afield than Darlington, while another person in the village is the only member of her family of four siblings who does not suffer the effects of inbreeding.

There are many interesting characters in this village and we soon become fond of all those who allow us to get to know them. One family in particular stands out. Alfie's family communicates with no one. Alfie works on the farm on the south side of the road (all the other houses, apart from the church lie on the north side). He and his wife, two adult daughters and one son-in-law live together with their young granddaughter, in a two-bedroom cottage, hidden away among the trees, beside the old water mill on the banks of the River Pont. How they all fit into this tiny cottage we will never know.

We take possession of the house three days before Christmas 1970, and so a new chapter begins in our lives. We now become a part of 'Northumberland', rather than belonging to the somewhat shifting population of the 'suburbs'. The people we are introduced to have, on the whole, been born and bred here. Their families have lived in Northumberland for generations. Society, at that time, was less mobile than it is today. Through various introductions from the Bosanquet family, we meet a more settled and less competitive society. In Ponteland, it mattered a great deal what you wore to pick the children up from school, how clean and tidy your house was, the quality of the cuisine when you entertained and what kind of car you drove. We fared pretty badly in all these categories. In the country, everything seems more relaxed and informal and I too begin to feel more comfortable.

As the children grow we are able to keep ponies and, eventually, a dog. The children can ride out alone on the country roads, cycle and play in the woods by the river. There is, perhaps, more freedom for children at a time when there seem to be fewer potential dangers. We become part of a rota with three other families to ferry the children to and from school; in our large estate cars, nine little girls are squeezed into the back: no seat belts in the 1970s! Mercifully, no one ever has an accident. The children are happy at this school and Miss Le Mare, the head teacher, is someone who inspires, and also recognizes the talents, of every one of her pupils. Our children adore her.

David's hours are now less grueling. He is at home for most of every weekend and is more available to his children. In 1974, he is finally appointed to a consultant post and we know that we will be able to stay in this house long-term and, possibly, forever. We begin making plans to enlarge and modernize it. For a year, we live among builders and rubble with everything continually covered in dust. By the end of the year our house is transformed into a light, warm, spacious and modern home with a beautiful red Aga to keep the kitchen cozy and warm throughout the year.

While the building is in progress, life carries on and the children are busy with their lives and friends. I am to take part in an opera; it is to be the first performance of an opera by John McCabe, with the composer himself conducting and overseeing the music. The libretto is based on a play by Bertolt Brecht called *Mother Courage*, in which the heroine, Mother Courage, is initially a young girl of 17; by the end she has grown into an old woman of 70.

I am to play the part of Mother Courage. From an acting point of view this is relatively challenging, but it is nothing compared to the complexity of the music! To learn an entire opera from memory with music that is entirely unmemorable is more of a challenge than anything I have undertaken before. It makes the difficulties of sharing the house with builders relatively unimportant! We are finally ready for the performances with the accompaniment of the Northern Sinfonia Orchestra; it is ultimately a tour de force, although I am not sure that the opera has ever been performed again!

Coinciding with the news that David has at last, at the age of 43, become a consultant, there is also a concern for his health. He and his colleague, Hugh Brown, are operating together one day when there is a cancellation on their morning list. Hugh suggests that he could remove an unsightly looking mole from David's leg. When the histology comes back it is diagnosed as a pre-malignant melanoma, so a large area of flesh has to be removed from the surrounding area and a skin graft from his thigh is placed over the damaged area. David has to be away from work for a few weeks while his leg heals. There is no further concern about the melanoma, but it arouses a sense of anxiety; the future somehow seems less certain.

But David's convalescence is a good time for us all. Not only does it give him time to adjust to the new responsibilities of being a consultant, but it also gives the children a rare opportunity to have leisure time with their Dad. He is so seldom available to them. Later, one of his greatest regrets is that over the years he had so little time for his children.

So, our lives continue: the children's lives are taken up with school, friends and ponies, David's life is mainly centered around work and I have an increasingly busy concert schedule. This includes recitals, opera, oratorio and a series of concerts in schools. I perform as part of a trio with two members of the Northern Sinfonia Orchestra - Alan Fearon playing the keyboard and Graham Evans playing the clarinet. We travel around the north of England giving concerts to music societies and local music organizations, fitting the concerts in around the busy schedule of the Northern Sinfonia. There are also broadcasts on Radio 3 with my accompanist, Alison Gordon, a wonderful musician and solo pianist.

Life continues relatively smoothly at home but there are a few tensions among the girls with their inevitable teenage problems. These occur mainly between Nicola and Helena. As sisters they have never really found each other's company easy to cope with. Could it be partly due to there never having been enough time or attention to go around? If only we had devoted more time to listening and trying to understand the problems that are a part of growing up. It is easy now to see how it could have been different, but sadly it isn't possible to go back and do it all again!

During these teenage years, we are very closely connected to a family who come to live near us, in Dalton House, a fine old stone house in our village and at one time, the dower house to Dissington Hall. Anna and Edward represent for our children the way parents should be. They have unlimited time for their children and give them unstinting support in everything they do. Cathy and Amanda have been close friends since Cathy was 3 and Amanda 4. Cathy prefers the Trevelyan Family to her own; in fact she even calls Anna and Edward, 'Mummy and Daddy'. Amanda also spends much of her free time with us. Nicola and Rosy Trevelyan share a passion for wild life, and birds in particular, and are often invited out together on bird-watching expeditions by a fanatical bird-watcher, called Ruth. (They are both now in prestigious jobs involved with conservation). The Trevelyan children become like an extension of our own family, especially their youngest son, Hugh, when he is small. So, in many ways our families become intertwined and the friendship between Anna and me has lasted for more than half our lives. We once rather rashly said to one another that we didn't want to live beyond 80. Having recently reached that age, we are inclined to feel another few years might not be a bad idea! So, for many years, we have shared our lives, our children and our hopes and fears, and Anna and Edward have been a loyal and generous support to us through our times of difficulty and bereavement. We have, in the past, shared many birthdays and Christmases as well as weddings and we continue to see one another whenever it is possible, although the family moved away from their house in Dalton when the children left home and it became too big to manage.

So, the Trevelyan family become an important part of our world. During the next eight years we are each busy in our various ways and little changes. Nicola is absorbed with her beloved pony, Mickey, who dominates her teenage years until she turns 15 and discovers boys! The pony is then unceremoniously handed on to Cathy, who doesn't yet know how to ride!

This is a major watershed in Nicola's life. She had earned Mickey with her life's blood when she was only 10. David was reluctant to embark upon the pony world foreseeing weekends spent driving around Northumberland with a horsebox in tow. However, Nicola's determination triumphs and David finally relents, saying she can have a pony when she has earned enough money to pay for the tack.

As our friends, the Dobsons, graze their ponies in our field, they offer to pay Nicola 50p a week if she will feed and water the ponies throughout the winter. This means getting up at 7.00 am on a winter morning, breaking the ice in the water trough when necessary and taking the two ponies their nets of hay. No one ever has to remind her to do this. Perhaps she also earns a little more from cleaning the tack.

By the end of the winter, she has earned enough -

together with saved pocket money and birthday presents - to buy a second-hand saddle and bridle, for the princely sum of £38.00. By this time, Sarah Dobson has outgrown her pony and Mickey belongs to Nicola at last. We realize that with this degree of determination and persistence Nicola will be able to achieve whatever she sets her heart on in life. And so it has turned out to be!

Helena also has an all-consuming passion, which is to own a dog. Again, we put every kind of obstacle in the way, saying that she would tire of the dog and that it would ultimately be her parents who would have to feed, train and walk him. Finally, David sets her an even more difficult task: she must avoid all conflict with Nicola for six months, irrespective of the provocation. To our astonishment she succeeds in this and for six wonderful months, peace reigns in our house!

On our way home from Canada that summer David drives us to a farm in Yorkshire where there is a bitch with four puppies. Helena has no hesitation in selecting Tasso, the boldest and most attractive of the litter. As we prepare to drive away, the farmer says to Helena, 'If this dog doesn't prove to be obedient it will be your fault, not his.' He adds that both Tasso's parents have been prize-winning sheepdogs.

Our problem lies not in teaching Tasso to be a prize sheepdog but in training him *not* to round-up sheep: fields of sheep surround our house and in spring there are lambs. Our neighbour, farmer Cliff Straughan, says Tasso will be a dead dog if he ever finds him with the sheep and suggests that he will put him with the 'tup' when Tasso is old enough, in order to deter him. Putting a young dog with a ferocious ram is either kill or cure. It works, and apart from a single occasion when Tasso very skillfully gathers a herd of sheep emerging from a van and successfully guides them into the field, (as we are on our way around Lake Coniston), he never again attempts to chase sheep. The instinct is so strong, and the skill bred in him runs so deep. The farmer is impressed and asks us how much we would like for Tasso, but he is not, of course, for sale. As he is bred to be a working dog he may be somewhat wasted as a pet. Nevertheless, Tasso becomes an important member of our family and he is never in any doubt as to which of us is his mistress!

Helena and I attend weekly dog training classes that winter and Helena takes responsibility for Tasso's training. Although he is too nervy and excited to perform well in class, when Helena reinforces the training at home, his swiftness to learn and his almost instant obedience are amazing. He exercises his instinct for rounding up sheep by endlessly gathering the ponies, who don't appear to mind. In fact, a strong relationship develops between Tasso and the horses and they became his raison d'être. The nice young woman who runs the classes is, however, less than impressed. Tasso's instinct to herd is turned towards all the other dogs in the class, which does not please the trainer! She scolds him each time he transgresses, shouting; 'You dirty little back street mongrel.' Although it is said in jest, Tasso takes it to heart and grovels on his back in abject distress, looking up at her with pleading eyes, until she laughs and orders him to get up. Dogs seem so eager to please from an early age.

We have many lovely holidays during the children's teenage years. We spend one summer in the beautiful Barbadian home of Jill Walker, David's sister, who is a well-known artist in the Caribbean. There we have the unusual experience of being looked after by the Walkers' maids, gardeners, chauffeurs and above all by their lovely cook, Eslin. Whenever I get up from the table to help clear the dishes I am reprimanded by Eslin who says, 'We don't do that here, mistress.' How easy it becomes to allow oneself to be waited on! Jill and Jimmy invite us to use their home in the West Indies while they have their annual holiday in their house in Scotland.

Then we are in Canada once again, with Meg and family, when the girls have a chance to be with their much-adored Canadian cousins, Christoph, Richard and Adi, who become like the brothers they always longed to have.

We have a memorable holiday camping beside a beach at Gairloch in Wester Ross, Scotland. The sun never ceases to shine, the sea and sky are the bluest of blue and the distant Cuillin Mountains of Skye rise grey and imposing on the horizon. We have with us a Mirror dinghy and a rowing boat; each day we go out to the surrounding islands, catch mackerel on our spinners and cook them on an open fire for supper. We explore the uninhabited islands and on one occasion we are just in time to see a seagull hatch from its egg, the nest concealed in a hole in a rocky outcrop.

In the evenings, when the children are in their tent ready for bed, David reads aloud to us from the evocative and perhaps *original* cowboy book, '*The Virginian*', by Owen Wister. When I reread that book, I can still hear his voice and am back in those wonderful youthful days when we were all still together. This holiday is an unforgettable time for us all.

But the children also have their own separate adventures. Pa Crockford has offered each of the girls a solo trip overseas when they are 11 years old, just before they need to pay for a full 'plane fare. Nicola chooses to go alone to Canada and Helena to Barbados; they are both destinations they have been to on family holidays and the families with whom they will stay are ones they know well.

Catherine, on the other hand, decides to go further afield to visit my half brother Christopher and his family - none of whom she has ever met - in New Zealand. David and I are concerned about her going so far, but she remains undaunted. She will spend Christmas with them and will be gone for three weeks. The flight takes over 24 hours.

I send her off with a rucksack full of little parcels; an

extended Christmas stocking. Each parcel contains something that will occupy her: a game, puzzle, crayons, a book and so on. There is one parcel for every hour, when she isn't sleeping. The parcels make the time slip by and the air stewardesses are attentive and kind. Catherine arrives to a great welcome from the Baynes family and feels immediately at home; Lorna gives her an enormous hug on arrival and her twin cousins, Hugo and Hilary, who are 15, are delighted to have a younger 'sister' they can knock about a bit, being the youngest in their family of eight. When Cathy sees the familiar muesli and brown bread I have always made she feels she has flown across the planet simply to arrive at home. She doesn't suffer from a moment's homesickness.

The Family

Helena with Meg

Chapter 14

Another Chapter

> *Twilight and evening bell,*
> *And after that the dark*
> *And may there be no sadness of farewell,*
> *When I embark;*
>
> *For tho' from out our bourne of Time and Place*
> *The flood may bear me far,*
> *I hope to see my Pilot face to face*
> *When I have crossed the bar.*

(Tennyson)

Every February, David and I spend a few days on our own in the Lake District and Mrs Stevenson - or Stevie as she is known to us - comes to hold the fort. These weeks together are times for re-connecting: time to talk, wander and think only of one another. These are rare and beautiful interludes in our full and ever-busy lives.

David's work has always taken precedence and I have also been inclined to take on too much and to become too preoccupied in my world of music, endlessly preparing for the next concert. To have a whole week of uninterrupted time together is special for us both. These are moments when we feel at peace with the world and with one another.

During the winter of 1978-9, Northumberland had a fall of snow greater than any in living memory. We were unaware of it because we were in Borrowdale at the time and there was no snow in the Lakes, beyond a sprinkling on higher ground. We had no 'phone contact (it was before the age of mobile 'phones) and we arrived back to find that the country road leading from the military road to Stamfordham had been completely blocked by more than 10 feet of snow.

The day of our return was the first day it had been possible to negotiate the country roads; a narrow path had been cleared through the snow, which was just enough space for a car to pass. Beside the cleared tracks were 15 feet piles of snow. The journey home was hazardous; we were the only vehicle on the road. At the top of the road leading to Dalton there was a 20' drift by Windy Walls farm; a local tractor had ploughed a narrow path through the snow so at last we were able to reach home.

We arrived to find our daughters jubilant and excited by the adventure of it all. Mrs Stevenson, indomitable as ever, had coped splendidly and the children had enjoyed a week's holiday from school. The oil had run out so there was no central heating and no Aga, so Stevie had lit the oil heaters and cooked sausages on an open fire in the sitting room. It was just like camping and the week had been one of endless fun in the absence of school and parents. Stevie and the girls had played many games of whist by a blazing fire, gambling with smarties. And the snow had provided boundless entertainment. So evidently, we hadn't been missed!

The outside world had simply come to a halt. Our neighbour, Cliff Straughan, arrived on his tractor to clear the driveway and Miss Hague from Broomy Hall, the house lying just beyond the village, walked to all the Dalton houses to deliver milk. It was wartime spirit all over again, with everyone pulling together. When the snow finally melted and things returned to normal, the children were rather sad.

I now jump to the winter of 1981. As usual, we have explored the lakes and hills surrounding Borrowdale, Watendlath and Haystacks and we have even attempted to walk up Scafell Pike. The days are bitterly cold and the waterfall at High Force is completely frozen. We are walking down from Watendlath one day, struggling to find the path due to a mist that has descended and obliterated all visibility. It is then that David tells me he is suffering from a pain in his abdomen, which has been there for some time. He hasn't done anything about it, hoping that the pain would go away. But it has persisted and is getting more pronounced. He clearly doesn't want to make me anxious, but I realize that he is more worried than he pretends. I say that he must get it checked as soon as we return home.

Perhaps something in him didn't really *want* to know. Instead of arranging an appointment with an abdominal surgeon he went to visit an old pal who was a physician. The various consultations continued over the following months and it wasn't until he finally had a barium enema, in June, that the large cancer in his bowel was discovered. Until that point the physicians had not carried out any tests and had treated him for spastic colon, which is a stress-related condition.

David knew that his life was at stake when the results came back, although he still wasn't aware of possible secondaries. But in retrospect, I think he did already know that this was likely. He spoke later of an enlarged gland in his neck, which he could feel, and which warned him of the possibility that the cancer had already spread to the lymphatic system.

In July a colleague at the RVI operated on David. I was at home when the 'phone rang. It was the surgeon, Mr. McNiel, ringing to tell me that David was still on the operating table and that the cancer had spread widely. He could only remove the tumor in the sigmoid area of the large intestine, but no further treatment was possible. It felt as if my world was about to come to an end. I answered the 'phone in my bedroom and came out of the room in shock. Nicola was on the landing. She asked about the 'phone call and I told her. She hugged me, and we wept together. I was suddenly aware of an astonishing maturity in her; in that moment she was comforting me and not thinking of herself.

I then went downstairs where my Mum was dealing with

the latest picking of raspberries. I told her the news. There was no reaction. She continued picking the raspberry beetles from the fruit. It was as if she simply couldn't take in this fresh disaster facing her family. I couldn't sleep that night. When I visited David after the operation, he was too drowsy to respond.

The following day I went to the surgical ward where most of David's patients were treated, so he knew all the staff well. He had learned that morning from the surgeon that he had only 6 months to live. To my surprise, he looked radiant, as though he had just heard the most wonderful news. His faith in God was the mainspring of his life. Now he felt as if he no longer had to struggle along on his own, carrying the weight of the world - as well as his patients' well-being and survival - on his shoulders. It felt like a reprieve from an impossible burden; it was a situation that he could do absolutely nothing about. He could simply allow things to take their course. I was totally baffled by his response. The hospital chaplain arrived, and they prayed together. David simply put everything - his whole life and his survival - into the hands of God.

David spoke of the 'fragmentedness' of his life and of his overwhelming tiredness as he had attempted to hold everything together. He said, 'It is as though the separate strands of my being have now become the rope of my totality.'

After ten days in hospital he came home to recover from the operation. For the first time in our lives we had long leisurely days together. It was, perhaps, the first and only time we had had unlimited time to talk and to try to understand what was happening to us. It was July and the weather was lovely. The children were on holiday and away from home for much of the time. We moved a bed into the garden where he lay under the cherry tree. Time seemed to stand still.

David had been a man of action, essentially a practical

man who had not wondered too much about the deeper aspects of life. Now he had time to read, think and wonder about life's meaning. Why one might become ill and about what *reasons* lie behind illness.

He began to wonder about himself. He hadn't spent much time being introspective, but he became aware of his own depression during the previous six months. One day, as he was driving home from work - he had just been reading about the early death of a colleague – he found himself thinking, 'Lucky devil, he's found a way out.' To think that death might be 'a way out' had come as a shock to him. Now it was a reality.

While he was having these thoughts, he heard about a couple in America who had written about a revolutionary way to treat cancer. The book is called *'Getting Well Again'* by Carl and Stephanie Simonton. They associated cancer with depression and reasoned that a depression of mood causes a depression of the immune system. When this happens, the cancer cells that are normally dealt with by the lymphatic system have a greater opportunity to multiply. The Simontons maintained that there is a psychological as well as a physical reason for all illnesses. One needs to ask, 'Why do I need this illness? What inner or emotional need am I not attending to?' For David, as a surgeon, this was a revolutionary way of thinking.

He began to look at his own life and the extent to which fulfilling a huge expectation, or duty, had been its driving force. His parents had both placed enormous expectations on him, though perhaps not consciously. They had longed for a son and when Pa decided two daughters was enough he drew the line at further children. But Ma took things into her own hands. After she became pregnant for a third time, she moved to a separate bedroom. That was the way things were for the rest of their married life.

Ma booked herself into a London clinic for the confinement, so that Pa would have nothing at all to do with the birth. She *knew* that she would have a son, and this was to be *her* son. From the word go David had to be something very special for them both. Ma had visions of him becoming a missionary doctor and going out to darkest Africa to save souls as well as bodies. Dad wanted him to become the surgeon he himself had always longed to be. David tried his whole life to fulfil both of their ambitions for him; life became too serious and made impossible demands on him. Perhaps David now perceived his own family as another source of burden and anxiety.

These days of recuperation brought with them an amazing sense of release, as though we were all freed from this invisible burden of needing to fulfill unspoken and impossible demands. While he was recovering from the operation, David's work at the hospital had to be divided between the other members of the team. Michael Black, the junior surgeon at the time, took on this task. He discovered that David, who had been responsible until now for sharing out the workload, had appropriated the lion's share and was, single-handedly, trying to reduce the unwieldy waiting list. When Michael appreciated the colossal amount of work David had undertaken, he commented, 'It's a killer,' before he realized what he had said. Indeed, it *was* a killer!

During the month that David took off work we went on holiday to a house overlooking Loch Ness, which belonged to friends of Johnny and Ann. I have said little about my lovely sister in law, who has been a true and lovely sister and friend to me over the years. Always a wise and sympathetic listening ear when things have been tough as well as a real practical support in giving a home from home to my daughters, especially to Helena, for whom at one time Johnny and Ann's home near Guildford became a welcome refuge. Ann has grown over the years and has been able to grow through the various family crises that have assailed them. She is someone of extraordinary resilience, strength and loyalty and I feel deeply indebted to her. For Johnny, she has provided not only an exceptionally beautiful home but also the loyalty and stability that has been so important for him.

Nicola wasn't happy during that holiday; perhaps she was more aware than her sisters that this was to be the last holiday with her beloved Daddy. It was a time of recuperation; we lay in the sun and David read to us from the book by Fynn called *Mister God, this is Anna.* Knowing what little time we had left as a family seemed to add extra meaning to the wonderfully profound and simple truths expressed by little four-year-old Anna. It is a book that has been important to us all; Cathy has even named her son, Fynn, after the author and Nicola's eldest daughter is called Anna.

David returned to work at the end of August, around the time of his 51st birthday. Nicola was busy raising money to go on the BSES (British Schools Exploring Society) expedition to Greenland the following year. She needed to raise £1,400, which was a huge sum in those days. She was given a place on the expedition partly because she was the third generation to apply. Pa had gone on the very first expedition as the doctor - and continued going for several years afterwards – and David had been to Lapland with the BSES when he was at Rugby. So, Nicola would be the first 3rd generation participant. Raising the money, in addition to the hard work for her 'A' level exams, meant that she was fully occupied. Her heart was wholly involved at the time with Mark, her first important boyfriend, which perhaps helped to take her mind off the inevitability of losing her Dad at the very time when she would be needing him most.

Life continued for a while as though everything had returned to normal. Every now and then David would make a remark which showed he was aware that there wasn't much time left. A man came one day to collect our car. David commented, 'I wonder what he would think if he knew he was talking to a dying man?' At the time I thought this was a little over dramatic, but it was, in reality, the truth. His time *was* running out. But, because our lives had returned to normal, it was hard for us to believe that there was so little time left.

David became ill in November. At first, he was able to take part in normal family life and every morning he would walk the mile to the nearby farm, Windy Walls, and back, before breakfast. He was losing weight and began to look like an ill man. Knowing that we had little time, he tried to instruct me about the things I had relied on him for: he showed me his meticulous accounts, which accounted for every penny spent, and he showed me how to work and maintain the mowers and other garden machinery. Gradually, he became too tired to do very much and would spend much of the day in bed, rising only for brief periods when he felt strong enough.

A week before Christmas David could no longer eat. For some time he had been suffering from nausea and anorexia and had lost nearly two stone in weight. He went into the RVI where he was once again in ward 5 - his own ward - which happened to have a St Thomas' trained sister. This was a bad time for him. It felt so much like the end. The doctors inserted a central line drip so that he could be fed, and he began to need larger doses of morphine to control the pain. He called this time, 'the dark night of the soul' and for the first time he felt unable to pray. He spoke of the sense of helplessness in relation to his experience of being a patient, when you are no longer in charge of your own life, commenting, 'You have no idea of the totally depersonalizing effect hospital can have.' It was as though, for a time, he lost himself. I thought that if hospital affects David in that way, when he is surrounded by familiar people in a familiar place, what must it be like for everyone else?

Cousin Adi was with us for Christmas that year. I went into Newcastle on Christmas Eve to do all the shopping and to buy the turkey. We all went to the midnight service at Matfen church and the children played with Adi in the snow as though nothing was amiss. Children have a wonderful ability to live in the moment and continue the normality of life. Ma and Pa came over on Christmas Day, laden with gifts and delicious things to eat. Somehow, we managed to make Christmas happen; having Adi with us made all the difference.

On New Year's Day, David came home. Our neighbours, Walter and Mary Fortune, greeted the ambulance as it came down the drive with a great bouquet of chrysanthemums. David was then carried on a stretcher to our bed. All the children were there to welcome him home. Mrs Stevie had come to stay, to look after the children and cook for us, so that I could devote my time to nursing David during the last few days of his life.

It was bitterly cold, in fact the coldest week on record. The temperature dipped to as low as 26 degrees centigrade below zero. Snow had fallen, followed by a deep frost. The countryside had been transformed; the snow on the rooftops and the feathered branches looked exquisite against an ice-cold sky. I was with David throughout the day and was able to attend to him at night. I had to feed him through the central line and he needed regular injections of morphine to control the pain. By now he was very weak and had the appearance of someone close to death.

In the months before he succumbed to the cancer David had practised visualization, as recommended by the Simontons' book, in the belief that such positive thinking can actually affect the growing tumor. But he no longer had the strength to fight it. It was as though, during those last few days, we had both given up the hope of a miracle and we were preparing for death.

Before he went into hospital, David had rung the Alnmouth Friary to ask if they knew of a faith healer, which was possibly more for us than for him. They said they could recommend someone who had helped one of their brothers, if we didn't mind the fact that he was Irish and a Roman Catholic. We were happy about both, if only he could help us! I rang Father Sean Conaty to ask if he would come, but he replied that his car had been vandalized and he had no means of transport. I offered to collect him, so he described where he lived in Long Benton, which was one of the roughest areas in Newcastle. The snow had been cleared from the main roads but there was ice on the minor roads so conditions were treacherous. I found his Church with the presbytery next door; Father Sean was waiting for me. On the way to Dalton he didn't talk much but just wanted to know a little about David and his illness.

David had come downstairs and was waiting for us in the sitting room. He spoke of himself, of his illness and of his belief that faith can heal a person, although he had no experience of it himself. He also spoke of his own faith. Then Father Sean spoke about himself, of the years he had spent in Chile and how he discovered there that he had the gift of healing, simply because doctors were so scarce. His parishioners had come to him for healing rather than to a doctor. He told me that sometimes it worked with people who have no faith and didn't work at all with others who have deep faith. It was impossible for him to tell when and with whom it would work. He said he had taken his vows of celibacy nearly 50 years before, 'And, thank the Lord, I have managed to keep my vows.' It was as though they both laid all their cards on the table. Father Sean prayed with David and later I drove him home. That night, for the first time, David was completely free from pain.

Soon after this, Sean's car was repaired. He then visited David every evening. Sometimes he didn't arrive until after midnight. He prayed with him and with us both; it was important to us that he didn't avoid the subject of death or try to jolly us along, in the way that our dear friend, Bishop John Ramsbotham, who had been giving David communion, tended to do. We were aware of how few people are comfortable addressing the subject of death, and yet it is what we needed; this was something that both of us were approaching and we needed help with facing it.

For Sean, death was just another aspect of the faith journey and it was something with which he felt quite comfortable. Little by little, David and I also began to accept it. The period when David came home to die was only a week, yet it had a quality of timelessness; a forever quality as though we had now entered a timeless zone. David asked me to put the clock where he could easily see it, as if his contact with time was gradually slipping away and he needed to keep his eye on it.

One night he had a dream that was so real, it felt as though the events had actually occurred. He saw a large number of people gathered together. They were all weeping. Then he saw a body being lowered into a grave. He suddenly recognized the body as his own. It was like a premonition and it seemed that his unconscious mind was preparing him for what was about to happen.

We both knew that we were near the end, yet David was still in full command of himself. The day before he died he got up to go to the loo. On the way to the bathroom he fell, lost consciousness and wet himself. As he came round he said to me, 'Surely you must know, Diana, that when someone faints you should raise their legs above their head?' He was a doctor to the last!

Father Sean came to the house again that night. I greeted him downstairs and he said, 'Sometimes, Diana, a person is ready to die, and it is difficult if those he loves are holding on to him. Perhaps now is the time to let him go?' He suggested that I go to David and tell him that it was now time to move on. Sean opened the Bible at random and read out a passage from the Song of Songs:

I opened to my beloved; but my beloved had withdrawn himself, and was gone: my soul failed when he spoke: I sought him, but he gave no answer.

(Song of Solomon: 5:6)

We went upstairs together. I told David that Sean had suggested he was now ready to leave and that I must let him go. Then Father Sean prayed with him. Later, Sean told me what had passed between them. David had asked him two questions; 'Father, what is faith?' Sean had answered, 'Faith is holding on' then, 'And what is freedom?' Sean answered; 'Freedom is letting go.' When Sean was leaving, he said: 'There's a really great man.'

And that night, David died.

David knew that he would not be with us in the morning. Before he went to sleep he said to me, 'Tonight, Diana, it would be best if you were to sleep on the floor, for tomorrow you will need all your strength.' So that is what I did. When I woke in the morning, he was gone.

I rang Ma and Pa, who said they would come straight over. It was remarkable to me, considering what David meant to them both, that their concern and outpouring of love was all for us that morning. On the 'phone Ma said, 'You poor, poor darling. This is so hard for you.' When they arrived later that morning Dad was immediately thinking about how he could help us practically, with things such as the car, finances and the garden. My father-in-law became a constant and real help to us all and took over the role of father to the children, especially to Nicola, who was very much in need of a father figure as she was about to launch into adult life. He commented to me that morning, and it was the only time I ever saw him weep, 'I have lost my closest friend.'

David's funeral was held on a day of deep frost and snow. Few people were able to get there, apart from those who lived locally. The moment that Johnny heard the news, however, he boarded a 'plane, flew north and helped me plan the funeral. He was a wonderful support, both practically - he even paid for the funeral - and emotionally. He read the lesson -

1Corinthians 13 - most movingly and beautifully. I don't think I could ever have got through that terrible time without his help. He was also a great help to the girls and made us feel that life would, somehow, continue.

After David's death, Father Sean continued to visit. He would sit with us beside the fire in the sitting room while the children asked his advice in relation to their lives. Nicola wanted to know whether or not one should take one's cue in life from one's peers; should she sleep with a boy just because it was expected, whether she felt like it or not? Sean's advice, which she took to heart, was never to do anything that doesn't feel right just because it is expected, or, as a result of peer pressure.

We were showered with kindness. Northumberland rallied round and we had more invitations than we could cope with. The bleak reality of David's absence and the forever-ness of it only dawned gradually. Perhaps this is nature's way, so that one isn't overwhelmed: life had to go on. The children's holidays ended; it was back to school with 'A' levels pending for Nicola and GCSEs for Helena. We had to eat, keep house and shop. Life just carries on. Perhaps it was helpful that I still had the children at home and that I had concerts to prepare for. Our daily concerns made us aware that there *is* life after David, although it felt like a bleak sort of life.

In the last week of David's life we had discussed the future. We had also spoken of his regrets, particularly the fact that he had never had enough time to spend with his daughters, because work had dominated everything. He told me that I was not the kind of person who would do well on her own and he made me promise that I would one day marry again. At the time that prospect seemed more unlikely than anything I could imagine!

Helena

Catherine

Chapter 15

Life Continues

That he who many a year with toil of breath
Found death in life, may here find life in death.

(Coleridge: *Epitaph for Himself.*)

Nicola celebrated her 18th birthday the summer following David's death, (1982). The Trevelyan family allowed us to use their home, Dalton House to give a concert and party for all those people – about 60 in total - who had donated money towards her Greenland adventure. My two colleagues, from the Northern Sinfonia, Allen Fearon and Graham Evans, agreed to give a concert, together with Graham's daughter, Bridget, who was a fine 'cellist, and also Simon and Kate Miller's daughter, Clara, who sang Schubert's *Shepherd on the Rock*. After the concert everyone came over to The Cottage for drinks on the lawn and a buffet supper. It felt like a celebration and also, a 'thank you', to everyone who had overwhelmed us with kindness and hospitality since David's death.

Simon Miller, an old friend from Bryanston days, who was now professor of anatomy at Newcastle University, helped Nicola gather all the equipment she needed for the expedition and she spent weekends training in the Lakes, practising Eskimo rolls in preparation for the kayaking she would be doing among the ice flows of Greenland. There was so much preparation to be done and she had had little training for the enormous physical challenges that lay ahead. In a moment of despair, she said to me, 'I just need my Dad. The kind of help I need just now you can't give me.' The expedition took place in August; her remit was to do research into the bird life of Greenland. It stretched her in every way: physically, emotionally and intellectually. She returned with greater confidence and renewed self-assurance in terms of her stamina and physical abilities. The people she met on that expedition were to become life-long friends.

After Greenland, Nicola never really lived at home again; she found it too difficult. She spent her year out between school and University living in the house of James and Joy Cadbury, which became a home from home. James was then head of research at the RSPB and through him she was able to spend the best part of a year working at their headquarters in Sandy and at various nature reserves around the UK. The Cadburys were endlessly hospitable to her. Through James' introductions and invitations to accompany him to research meetings, she got to know most of the people who would later interview her for jobs. Nicola's year with the Cadburys proved to be of great significance in terms of her future career. They also gave her the support she desperately needed after the loss of her beloved Dad.

At home, we struggled on. Helena wanted to try for a place at the University of Oxford and a kind friend, Allison Gardner-Medwin, came to us in the evenings to give her extra tutoring. This was good for Helena's confidence; she also had individual coaching from her tutor, Mr Pruce, at school. She did well in her 'A' levels but in the end didn't make it to Oxford; perhaps Bristol was, for her, a better choice. During her 'A' level year Christoph decided to do his elective in medicine in Newcastle. He brought his family over from Canada to live with us for the six months of his stay. His wife, Yvonne, was accompanied by her mother who kept her company while Christoph spent long hours in the hospitals and she also helped Yvonne with the children: Fiona, who was 3 years old, and Vicky just 3 months. It made for a full and busy household!

Helena had decided to spend her year out as an au pair in France. An acquaintance of mine asked if she would like to go to some friends of hers who lived in the Château de Lude in the Loire Valley. The family was looking for 'an intelligent girl' who could look after the children and provide companionship for the Countess de Nicolay. The only snag was that Helena had absolutely no experience with small children! So, the evening before she was due to leave she asked Yvonne whether she could bath baby Vicky in the kitchen sink. This she managed successfully, with instructions from Yvonne, and she learned how to put on a nappy at the same time. This was the sum total of Helena's experience before she left for France to take on sole charge of the De Nicolay's two daughters: one was two years old and the other just two months. Somehow, miraculously, the children survived!

We had a letter from Helena soon after she arrived, saying, 'You know Mum, the dining room is so vast I couldn't even see to the other side.' And the size of the chandelier was a thing of wonder also. This is where they ate all their meals. Even taking into account Helena's short-sightedness, the proportions did seem impressive!

It was lonely at times in that great château and being in sole charge of such small children was exhausting. She had a bedroom in one of the castle's towers, and the children slept in their cots in an adjoining room. She was literally in charge of them for 24 hours a day. Her way of soothing the children if they were upset was to play Beethoven sonatas to them on the piano that had belonged to Chopin, which appeared to work like a charm. It was all valuable experience for becoming a mother herself. She survived it magnificently and in her spare time she was allowed to ride the family's splendid horses, which had been trained for the summer displays of Son et Lumière. Helena returned home speaking fluent French and she had developed a warm friendship with Barbara, the Countess, which continued after she left. She also found that she had a real delight in, as well as an unusually good empathy for, small children.

She went on to Bristol with new-found confidence.

Little by little we began to pick up the threads of our lives again. Before Helena left for France she had assumed a new position in the house. Nicola had always tended to dominate and with Nicola gone, Helena was now the eldest. She commented that without a Dad it was easier to be heard and that now, I was directing all my conversation to the children and sharing my thoughts and ideas with them. Suddenly, they seemed less like children and more like companions.

Helena had spent many hours with David over the summer while he was ill, and they had got to know one other in a new, perhaps more adult, way. She was deeply influenced by David's faith, which was something he has passed on to her. After David's death she commented, 'Having seen Dad die, I shall never be afraid of dying.' She had been thinking deeply and seemed old beyond her years.

About a year after David's death I drove to Reed House to visit my mother, because Johnny and Ann had gone on holiday to Ireland and she needed help. What I discovered, and what she had managed to conceal from everyone, was that she was simply not coping. She had developed Parkinson's – and had suffered from this for a few years – but I soon realized that she was also beginning to suffer from dementia.

I found that she was living on cornflakes and milk and that it could take her more than an hour to get dressed in the mornings. She was then so exhausted that she would have to return to bed. The stairs were steep, treacherous and without a bannister. She had to go up and down on her bottom, which took her a long time. Johnny and Ann, who lived no more than 100 yards away, were apparently unaware of her struggle. She was careful not to let them see how hard life had become because she feared being sent away to a home.

I suggested that she come home with me, to have a holiday in Northumberland, but I gathered her winter clothes and precious things because I knew she wouldn't be returning to Reed House again. Perhaps in some part of her, she knew this too. Just as we were about to set off - I had already started the car engine - she said; 'If you could just pop up to my bedroom and open the cupboard on the left, you'll see some books and a copy of the *Just So Stories.* In it you'll find some money.' I found over a thousand pounds tucked between the pages!

My mother lived with us in Northumberland for two and a half years, until her death on New Year's Day, 1985. After about a year she was no longer able to walk, so her days were spent in a wheelchair. We brought her bed downstairs to the room that had been David's study; from the bay window she had a view of the garden and enjoyed watching the birds and an occasional hedgehog. Her dementia gradually progressed until she needed full-time care. Two of the children were still living at home; they helped with her dressing and feeding, which was no hardship, as they loved her. She was always gentle and appreciative of everything. One time, when I was washing her in bed and getting her ready for the day, she said, 'Darling, this is so very kind of you. Do you do this for all your guests?' In her mind, she was with us for a brief holiday and would soon be going home to Reed House.

During the time that my Mum was living with us, I taught singing to the choral scholars and other gifted singers at Durham University. I was there for two to three days a week; teaching took place at Nicola's college, Trevelyan College, so we were often able to have lunch together in the dining room. As I don't play the piano the students would bring their own accompanist, usually an organ scholar, so I was also able to give tuition, (with regard to interpretation), to the accompanist. While I was working, the state provided carers and a district nurse came to give Mum a bed bath every morning.

But there was a time when it all became too much. It was

Easter and there had been no help for several days. I was pruning the roses in the rose garden; Mum was sitting in her wheelchair watching me. I said in exasperation, 'What is it that keeps you here?' Her reply was, 'It's love.' I understood her to mean that it was through our care for her that she was experiencing *being* loved. She had always been the one who had cared for everyone else.

However, I believe that she also knew when it was time to go. It was Christmas 1985 and she had shared Christmas Day with us and enjoyed her presents. I was sitting with her on New Year's Eve, opening a present to her that had been forgotten. I was exhausted. I said to her, 'Mum, we will not have any help next week. Would you very much mind going to stay in the War Memorial Hospital for a while?' After a pause she replied, 'I most definitely would!', and she died that night. Perhaps we really do have the ability to let go when there is no longer anything to live for?

Despite her dementia there was a part of my mother that remained very much aware, and she had moments of absolute lucidity. One day, our friend Simon Miller came to visit, as he often had done after David's death, to help with anything that needed doing. He went to Annema, who was sitting in the kitchen in her wheelchair and asked, 'How are things with you, Annema?' Her reply, quick as a flash, was, 'How the mighty are fallen.'

Somehow, despite her disability, she had a really lovely presence. Perhaps it was her ability to always see the very best in every situation. She didn't dwell on what she couldn't do or what life had taken from her. She enjoyed what life offered her to the fullest extent, even at the end of her life. Every morning she had a bowl of porridge; as she ate it she would say, 'This is paradise.' In the afternoon she would have a sleep and when she awoke it was morning again and she wanted breakfast, which meant another bowl of porridge and a second paradise. How many of us, in our full and varied lives, can experience paradise twice every day!

Part Three

Chapter 16

A Second Marriage

In 1982 I am a widow with three daughters, who are 18, 16 and 14 years old and all are still living at home. Our mutual friends, Margaret and Norman Dobson, invite me, together with a young man called Chris, who is a colleague of Norman's, to an Edwardian ball which is held for charity every year at the Newcastle Civic Centre.

First we have to learn the steps to the Quadrille and Lancers dances, so we meet at the house of our friends James and June Hill in Darras Hall, Ponteland, to practice. My partner for the evening is Christopher Jansen; everyone else has come as a couple. On this occasion we don't have much opportunity to talk, but I learn from the Dobsons that he has been on his own for some years since his wife died from breast cancer at the young age of 29, leaving him with four small boys to raise. He is a man of medium height, with a gentle, rather diffident manner. And he dances beautifully!

I leave the Hills' before everyone else to collect Helena from the Ponteland High School. She has been to London to see Othello, the play she is studying for 'A' level and has returned on the school bus. She asks me about the evening; I say I have been dancing with a widower who is the father of four sons. Without any preamble she simply says, 'Marry him.' However, I have been a widow for only 10 months and am certainly not thinking of marriage!

At the ball a few days later, Christopher talks to me

about his wife, Veronica, and his struggle in bringing up the boys single-handedly. The youngest son, Andrew, was only 18 months old when his mother died, which puts my own situation and widowhood into fresh perspective. I feel an immediate empathy for this young man. Christopher is just 43 years old and I am 44, but we both feel much older in terms of life experience.

Christopher drives me home after the dance and I invite him in, but he declines. I hear nothing more from him until the following year, when the Dobsons again invite us both to make up their party at the Edwardian ball. This time I remember a strong attraction between us; I love dancing with him and 'could have danced all night.' This time, he accepts the offer of hospitality when we reach my home. A series of invitations follows. I believe he invites me to four different events in the same week! My mother, who by then has been living with us for some time, comments, 'Don't you think he's rushing you a bit, darling!' There is a hunt ball, a works 'Christmas do' - he works as personnel manager for Stirling Organics chemical firm – where he doles out presents to the senior managers and the staff who are leaving. Finally, he asks me out to dinner at the General Havelock, an exceptional restaurant in Haydon Bridge. When I arrive at his home in Fourstones, noone answers the bell, so I just walk in through the open door. I find Chris watching television and don't recognize this bespectacled man at first, as he had been careful to remove his glasses for our previous meetings. I soon realize that he is quite severely short-sighted.

We have a lovely evening and I enjoy talking to him; our conversation is mostly about our families and our experience of widower and widowhood which, for me, is still very green. He speaks of Veronica and his love for her and the fact that she died so suddenly, in the full bloom of her youth and beauty. In some ways he has never recovered from this, although it is now about 15 years since her death.

He asks me if my marriage was a happy one. I simply say, 'It grew.' At the end of that evening we kiss one another for the first time and he comments, 'You have such sad eyes.'

I feel very much at ease with Chris and am especially moved by the courageous way he has coped with his loss. I find him unassuming and endearingly honest. He is always totally himself and isn't interested in trying to impress. In fact, quite the contrary. His view of himself is exceptionally low-key. When we speak of the things that interest us, I am left with the impression that he isn't interested in anything much, apart from the Army, which had been such an important part of his early life. He says that he doesn't read, isn't particularly interested in music, art, ideas, people, or study. I am left wondering what we would have to talk about and whether we would ever have anything in common. I later discover that he is well-read and has an amazing understanding of, and delight in, classical music. He is able to recognize the music of most classical composers, often after only a few bars – particularly Beethoven's symphonies.

For many years, Chris has been an eligible widower in Northumberland and has been out with many women. He has been on the hostess list as a rare single man, to even up the numbers at a dinner table. Until now, he has managed to evade every attempt by Northumberland hostesses to find him a partner.

The following weekend Nicola and I are invited to Fourstones for Sunday lunch. I discover that Chris is a fine cook and that he and Justin, his eldest son, make a splendid and well-rehearsed team in producing and serving the Sunday roast with all the trimmings. After lunch, Justin and Nicola disappear to talk to one another and Chris and I wash the dishes. Nicola later tells me that she commented to Justin on how lonely it must have been for his Dad, spending so many years by himself while his boys were away at boarding school. Justin's reply was simply; 'He has his solutions!'

Soon after this Sunday lunch, Chris and I walk to a local hill near our homes, known as Shaftoe Crags. At the summit of the hill is a cave with a wide rocky opening and a view to the south over a lovely stretch of Northumberland countryside: a hillside covered in bracken which leads to intensely green pasture and beyond the fields, a collection of stone buildings around an old farmhouse. In the distance we see the traffic, looking like dinky toys, on the A686, the Jedburgh road. We sit on a rock outside the mouth of the cave, watching the misty blue of the hills beyond the busy road and listening to the cry of a curlew in the distance.

Without warning, Chris asks me to marry him. I have just embarked on a degree course at Newcastle University as the first step in training to be a psychotherapist. The training was due to start in Newcastle in a year or two, and a degree was a mandatory requirement for acceptance on the course. Marriage wasn't really on the agenda! Chris doesn't require an answer at once, but he does add, 'I don't need a wife to iron my shirts, I've been doing that for years. I would want you to be able to fulfill yourself.' This was a totally different kind of proposal!

For a time I have been going out with a well-known cardiologist who Andrew Henderson had introduced me to, as well as a man I like very much, called John, who has taken me to the theatre and invited me to his estate in north Northumberland. John has also recently been widowed and is a shy and diffident man, but a lovely companion. He enjoys music and has come to several of my concerts to hear me sing. I am aware, however, that both men want and need a full-time wife to take over the management of the home and to be a charming hostess and helpmeet. I don't want to play that role again, so the thought of a husband who will help me to 'fulfil myself' is an attractive prospect!

In due course I accept Chris' proposal and we go out to dinner to celebrate. All our combined seven children dine together at my house while we are gone. We wonder how they will get on together. When we return, we find them all in a semi darkened sitting room with three girls sitting on the laps of three boys. I can't now remember which of the boys is without a partner! This seems to confirm the rightness of our coming together; it appears to be a unanimous decision!

Circumstances change, however, and Chris has the opportunity of a career change. He has thought for some time of moving to London, realizing that when all the boys have left their school, Ampleforth, they are likely to end up in the capital. The opportunity to become personnel manager at the Swiss Bank Corporation has arisen. He is successful in securing the job and this is a considerable promotion in terms of both status and salary. At first the Jansen family rent Reed House, which has stood empty since my mother came to live with us. It is a little bleak and scantily furnished, but it gives the Jansens a place to live until Chris is able to buy a house in London. Johnny and Ann are living next door, in a Swedish Scandia House they have recently had built.

Two years before we are able to marry, we have a sailing holiday in Turkey. It is a paradisal time and one which fulfils a long-held ambition for Chris to explore the lovely Aegean coastline, at the time still totally unspoiled. It is so wild and beautiful that we decide to go again the following year, this time together with Matthew, his girlfriend Natalie and Andrew. Chris suddenly gets cold feet after this holiday and calls the wedding off. I am devastated. It isn't possible to discuss with him what has gone wrong. He has made the decision to pull out - and that is that. I start going out with John again and we enjoy memorable walks together in the wilder parts of Northumberland. Then one day, out of the blue, Chris walks in through the kitchen door in Dalton. After this, there is no turning back.

We are at last to be married that summer, on August 29th,

1987. The marquee takes up the entire lawn in front of the house. All our children play a part in the wedding; Justin is best man, Matthew is the driver to and from the church, Simon reads the lesson and Andrew is the photographer. The three girls act as ushers in the church and then as hostesses at the luncheon after the service. Only a few of our friends are invited as we want it to be a celebration for our seven children. In the evening, we hold a splendid party for all our young with dinner and dancing and a jazz band which continues 'til dawn. Each of the young is given a guest list of 20; the total number of guests is approximately 200. Chris and I leave at 3.00 am and find our way, somewhat drunkenly, to a hotel at Three Lane Ends. The young continue to party until all the food runs out and the marquee is eventually dismantled.

Our honeymoon is the loveliest possible. We spend two weeks in a 38' sloop called Pristina, exploring the wonders of the Adriatic Coast, in Croatia. We work our way South from Kremik, a port not far from Split, and visit the beautiful towns of Hvar and Korcular with their Venetian style architecture. Everything about this holiday is enchanting. After all the ups and downs of our years of knowing one another, we seem finally to have come home. Perhaps Allan Higgs, the vicar who married us, expressed our doubts and misgivings when he said in his wedding homily, 'Perhaps both Chris and Diana will be feeling a sense of disloyalty in relation to their previous marriages, but that feeling will grow less in time and anyway, in heaven, we are all married to one another.' Chris had found this idea distinctly puzzling, but certainly, the ghosts of our previous loves and lives do, in time, become less present.

We live apart during the first year of our marriage; I am studying for my degree in Newcastle and Chris is now established in his job at the Swiss Bank. He has bought a house in Balham, where he lives with three of his sons; by this time, Justin has joined the army and is based at

Sandhurst. Cathy is a student at Newcastle University, studying to be a speech therapist and I am now in my second year in the department of Combined Honours, so we become fellow students!

Chris travels to Northumberland every Friday evening and returns to London on the 6.00 am train on Mondays. It works well for us both and particularly for Chris, who has been used to living alone and running his own life for nearly 18 years. It allows us to break in gently to the eventual possibility of sharing every aspect of our lives.

I make a wonderful friend while I am at Newcastle. Her name is Barbara Steel. She also has decided, late in life, to take a degree. We enter student life together and find ourselves in heated discussions with students the age of our children, with punk hair styles and raggedy jeans. When I am preparing for my final dissertation she is a willing audience while I speak my way through my research. The subject is *Jung as Symbol of the Self*. I receive valuable feedback from Barbara, and my writing begins to flow as a result of her encouragement and affirmation. Within ten days I have completed my dissertation.

Barbara and I support one another through difficult patches and the anxieties over exams. For Bar, studying requires the most extraordinary determination and discipline. In her first year her family moves to an old farmhouse that has had nothing done to it since 1903, and the year after that, her daughter, Sarah decides to get married. So, in addition to her studies, she has a wedding to arrange. She achieves everything magnificently and sails through her degree with a 2:1!

Bar is a true artist. It isn't long before she and Peter, together, have created one of the loveliest homes and gardens in Northumberland. The herbaceous borders curve down the sides of a gently sloping lawn; at the bottom is a large pond and wild garden which disappear into the beautiful, gently rolling Northumberland countryside beyond. The hemels of the original farm buildings make a splendid and totally sheltered area for climbing roses and tender plants. It is a lovely garden at any time of year.

I complete my degree in 1988. It has been a time of discovery and personal growth. I realize that studying is something I find exciting and fulfilling and not the uphill struggle it had often seemed to be at school. I do well in all my subjects; my professor, John Sawyer, later told me that I had missed a first by a whisker. But I do get a first in all my course work. From having been a very average student at school I am able now to recognize a newly acquired gift: the ability to think, both creatively and clearly! That is quite a surprise!

Chris and Diana at Diana's graduation

A friend of mine, Carlotta Johnson, was inviting some of her friends to contribute to a booklet called *Another Day has Westered*, about the experience of turning 50. I was one of the contributors. For me, passing the half-century mark was a watershed and a new beginning. I reflected on how it had felt after David's death. How, 'The possibility of life ever having meaning again seemed so remote.' I wrote that, 'Children at a time of sorrow are like arrows aimed towards the future, which they make a certainty.' I was reminded of Kahlil Gibran's *The Prophet,* in which he writes of children as the future:

'For life goes not backward nor tarries with yesterday.
You are the bows from which your children as living arrows are sent forth.'

My children taught me that there was indeed life after death. Suddenly I discovered intense pleasures in small things; the first snowdrops in spring and a sense of physically unfolding with the warmth of the sun. I remembered the joy I experienced on a day of sun, snow and sharp cold, with icicles hanging from branches and gutters. A sudden realization; 'I am alive.'

Then, in relation to my new training to become a psychotherapist, I wrote, 'I began to experience a new courage and a renewed trust in life (as) I embarked on training in another profession, from singer to psychotherapist.' The singer is so dependent on affirmation from without. In my own therapy, a mandatory part of the training, I discovered a new kind of affirmation, coming from inside myself. Life began to feel more secure. I understood what the priest (Father Sean), who helped us at the time of David's death and who helped him to die, had meant when we talked together at a subsequent meeting. I told him, 'I have lost my rock.' His reply was, 'I don't know how that feels, because no human being has ever been that for me. My rock is God.' What I experienced now was another kind of affirmation, which was no longer dependent on an audience.

There are two poems that I wrote at this time which seem to express the sheer surprise I felt at being alive.

A long way on.
A new wave
of life... of love.

A new sea, a new sun
seen for the first time.
Another spring.

My eyes opening
to find there is more
to being alive.

And again, written a little while later:

Such a strange feeling
of stepping off the world
into the unknown.

My unknown self
peeping through
and beckoning,

not sure yet
how far... how deep
I dare to travel

along this unfamiliar
path.

I felt I was at the beginning of life again. When I wrote this, I was already a qualified psychotherapist and had established a private practice in Newcastle. By this time, after five years of thrice-weekly therapy, which was necessary for the training, a lot of water had passed under our bridges and Chris and I had also navigated the teething troubles of a new marriage. At the end of these fifty-year old reflections, I wrote, 'It feels fine also to be married, and to be married to someone who is truly a companion; in other words, not just someone who shares my bread (com panis), but every aspect of my life. He has sustained and encouraged me through the rocky patches: finals, a new life, a new profession and the pitfalls of therapy! He has helped me to find an inner rock that I hope won't get swept away in the next storm.' I conclude with this final sentence, 'The sun is shining, once again the snowdrops are in bloom and it's good to be alive.'

I joined Chris, as well as various members of our joint family, in his London home in Balham, for the beginning of my training at the Westminster Pastoral Foundation. It was a five-day week and full on experiential training, during which we were, metaphorically, turned inside out. My therapy with Joel Ryce-Menuhin, (brother-in-law to Yehudi), kept me afloat, and as I struggled with my demons, I was often comforted by hearing the lovely strains of Yaltah Menuhin, Joel's wife, practicing the piano in the room next door!

Joel came from Chicago originally. He was a child prodigy and had been a concert pianist until he was in his 30's. He and Yaltah travelled the world together playing as a duo. During his 30's he suffered from a tendon problem in one of the fingers of his left hand, which meant it became impossible for him to continue to play the piano. After years of readjustment he finally trained as a Jungian analyst. For me, he was a life saver. He accompanied me on the most difficult and painful journey of my life, as I grieved with him over the death of a beloved father, brother and husband. So much unfinished business that needed to be negotiated and lived *through*. It was something I had never been able to do. Perhaps there was also historical unfinished business in relation to my mother's losses, as well as my grandmother's. All these unmourned losses that get handed on, from generation to generation. For a time, I was lost and disorientated, and Chris, with his wonderfully positive attitude and practical support, gave me the containment I was needing at that difficult time. Joel became for me the rock, the absolute and loving acceptance which allowed me to travel to a place, deeper and more vulnerable, than any I had dared to venture to before. He was there through thick and through thin, and with the help my of dreams, a tsunami of tears and of words as well as sandplay, we negotiated the rough and rocky seas of the unconscious, until I felt able to leave London and the support he had given me. I can never express in words my debt to him for the work we did together over those five years. Perhaps my need to train was really because, at some point, it was necessary for me to do this work…not only for myself, but also to free my children from a family backlog of unexpressed grief!

Chris was a magnificent support during these traumatic early months. He was working at the Swiss Bank Corporation in Gresham Street as their chief personnel officer. We commuted together each morning; while he got off at Bank, I continued to High Street Kensington, on the Circle Line.

He ran the house, catered for its varying numbers of occupants, did all the cooking and organized cleaning parties on Saturday mornings. I feel that he must have been the only Senior Manager at the Swiss Bank, sitting at his enormous and impressive desk in an office that would have housed all the family, who was still doing his own cleaning! It was what he had always done and he just continued doing it; the addition of a few more people seemed to be no problem! Sometimes, at weekends, we drove home to Northumberland; later on, it became easier to travel by train.

Although Chris was very stern with his own children, with the girls he treated any problems with a light and humorous touch. Helena did not feel it was necessary to spend her Saturday mornings cleaning her room. She spoke of it being a question of how high a threshold one had in relation to dirt. As mine was fairly low, it made sense that I should do the lion's share of the cleaning. Chris was coming down the stairs one Saturday morning. He heard an unfamiliar sound coming from Helena's room. He knocked on the door, and Helena, above the din, shouted for him to come in. He said: 'it's that music, such wonderful music', Helena replied; 'I didn't think you liked jazz Chris!' 'Oh no', he replied, 'it's the symphony of the hoover.' It was the first time Helena had been known to clean her room!

Before completing my time at The Westminster Pastoral Foundation, I began another period of training. It was possible to combine two trainings as it was only necessary to attend lectures for psychotherapy training once a week, on a Tuesday evening. I didn't mention to anyone that I was doing a second training, but it meant that when I eventually qualified and was able to return to work in Northumberland, I had acquired three separate trainings. Firstly, as a Jungian orientated psycho-dynamic counsellor, secondly as an analytical psychotherapist and thirdly, (as a result of my training with Ryce-Menuhin, who was the pioneer in London of sandplay therapy), as a Jungian sandplay therapist. I was able to see all my patients at home in Northumberland and was supplied with training patients from the NHS waiting list at the psychotherapy department at the RVI in Newcastle. As there was a shortage of qualified psychotherapists in the North East at the time, it meant I was able to complete the training requirements in record time.

I left London with great trepidation, to begin my practice in the north. For five years I had been receiving therapy three times a week and supervision twice a week. Now I was about to begin my practice in earnest without any support at all! Joel sent me on my way with the words,

'You've been having therapy and supervision for five years. Now you are fully equipped to manage on your own.' With Joel's belief in me, I somehow knew that all would be well. I worked from home and also had a consulting room in Westgate Road in Newcastle. It wasn't long before I had a full practice. I was later able to travel to Edinburgh once a month to have supervision with a wise and exceptional Jungian analyst called Bani Shorter, who helped me through many difficult patches.

In the meantime, Chris had left the Bank and had come home to work for the Tyne and Wear Development Corporation, in Newcastle. For Chris, it was a considerable drop in both pay and prestige, but he enjoyed the job and the great variety of people he met, and he loved being back in Northumberland. So, for a time all was well, and we were both absorbed in our work and our lives together.

Chris had energy to spare, so he set about improving our home. He enlarged the sitting room and built a large north-facing conservatory leading from the sitting room. Finally, he built a new wing to the west which he called, 'The Psychiatric Wing.' So this was where I practiced for the next ten years. He also built me a Sand House, next to the consulting room, and two sand trays with their mobile stands, so that I was able now to practise as the first fully qualified Jungian Sandplay Therapist in the North East. These were richly rewarding years for us both and I loved this partnership in which we supported one another with our work, with our two families and the problems that arose and with all the tasks in relation to our two homes.

Chris was able to give me both practical and emotional support for my work and I also felt physically cared for because Chris liked to do all the cooking, just as he always had done. It was so lovely for me to finish work with clients at 6.00 or 7.00 pm, smell the delicious aromas coming from the Aga then make my way to the kitchen and watch Chris as he created beautiful dishes: Indian, Italian and Chinese.

Once again, I was a child, watching my mother as she prepared our meals and anticipating the delicious food that I had had no part in preparing.

We shared all the tasks of our new life: in our French evening classes we learned the phrase, *nous partageons les taches,* and that is how it was in every aspect of our lives. One afternoon, early in our marriage, I was in the orchard mowing the long grass with our big Hayter machine while Chris was upstairs ironing a huge pile of shirts. We came together for a cup of tea and asked ourselves, 'Is this really the right way round?' Perhaps, in due course, Chris did more of the mowing and I took on some of the ironing! But both of us had been used to doing everything; there was no distinction between 'his' and 'her' tasks. This is how it continued to be.

I am reminded of a time, very early in our relationship, before we had become lovers. I said to Chris one day, when he was planning to stay the night, 'With me, it's all or nothing. Unless we are in it for the long term I would rather we didn't sleep together.' I had only ever had one lover, and that was David. Chris's response to this was, 'I see, so it's a package deal!' Thinking about it now, I wonder if he had realized then how big a package he was taking on!

Various members of our family came to live with us at different times, between jobs or marriages or as a result of illness, so we provided a secure base for our seven children when they needed one. Christmases in those early years were lovely, once more filled with young children as our young married and had families of their own, and everyone gathered at our home.

Chapter 17

France

After Veronica died, Chris received help from another army wife called Ruth Treays who lived with her family near by. Ruth took Chris' son, Simon, under her wing as a result of the friendship that had developed between Simon and her son Jeremy at their infant school. The friendship with the Treays family continued over the years; Ruth and her husband Peter would invite Chris and the boys to their summer home in the Dordogne. Chris once said to Ruth, 'You saved my life.' She was unobtrusively there for him and the family in so many ways. When Ruth and Peter left the North East, Simon continued to go and stay with them during the holidays and he referred to Ruth as, 'My surrogate mother.'

In the summer of 1995, Chris and I were invited to Becky Treay's wedding in the Dordogne. Ruth, and her twin sister Lib, told Chris that they had found the ideal home for us. At the time, we weren't planning to buy a house in the Dordogne. However, after the wedding we did go to look at the house they had recommended. It wasn't possible to look inside because a family was holidaying there; we simply viewed it and the small adjoining house from the road. From there we could also see the swimming pool situated between the two houses. Without further ado, we made the decision to buy it!

Later that autumn, Chris went to stay with the Dutch couple who owned the house, Herr and Frau Juten de Jong, and the whole transaction was completed over the course of a weekend. For the two houses, the large swimming pool and a hectare of land he paid 80,000 euros.

We took possession of the house at Christmas and were given a warm welcome by all the inhabitants of the hamlet of Le Mespoul. We gave a drinks party on Christmas Eve and all the neighbours arrived bringing gifts of produce. One farmer brought kindling and logs while another brought eggs and paté de fois gras. The patissier, Robert, and his wife, Jeanette, brought beautiful home-made chocolates. We felt we had been accepted in this tiny unspoiled area of rural France; before long, all the inhabitants of Le Mespoul became our helpers and friends. As none of them could speak any English, we soon became fairly proficient in French

The main house was called La Grange and had been converted from a barn. It consisted of one large room downstairs – this was the kitchen, dining room and sitting room combined. Everything took place in here. It had a large inglenook fireplace which was wide enough for a seat on either side of the fire. The grate could accommodate logs of 3' – 4' long.

Upstairs there was a master bedroom and three additional bedrooms, with space for another bed on the landing. The only bathroom and loo were downstairs. There was no central heating, so in wintertime we kept the log fire burning which spread its warmth throughout the house.

The smaller house was modern and had a similar arrangement downstairs, with three tiny bedrooms above. It was ideal for families with small children, so when our families joined us for summer holidays, the young with small children could have their own area and eating arrangements and we could all enjoy the outside space and swimming pool together. It meant, also, that if two families wanted to holiday together they could each have their own house. It worked well and we had many wonderful holidays with all our families and their children. Summers were a social whirl, with the Treays families and their many friends creating an endless round of alfresco dinners and parties.

Our house was situated at the highest point of the hamlet; it commanded a view over the valley towards woodland and a forest of acacia trees, splendid in the spring with their white blossoms. On summer evenings we ate our supper outside, looking down over the valley. There was no sign of habitation apart from one or two distant lights: we would watch as the stars multiplied above us, brilliant against the dark sky. These were moments of absolute silence and peace when I experienced a sense of being removed from all the cares and worries of the world. I enjoyed a relaxation of mind, body and spirit that I have never experienced so totally anywhere else. The times we spent there were serene and lovely: after a week of unwinding we would forget about time, stop wearing our watches, wake when we felt like waking and eat when we were hungry. Time took on a different aspect; a sense of timelessness.

Among the many friends we enjoyed spending time with during those lovely holidays were Lib (Ruth's twin sister), and her G.P. husband, Duncan. We had splendid walks together and one year explored the Pyrenees, with Duncan and Lib in their camper van and Chris and me staying at nearby hotels. Lib and I had much in common. Both of us were working as psychotherapists and we both had three daughters. There was never a shortage of things to talk about! One year, we spent Christmas together at our house in the Dordogne; the first Christmas we had spent without any member of our families. It was strangely peaceful - no presents, cards and minimal decoration. It was a relief to have a change from the usual exhausting hurly burly of normal Christmases.

Many friends came to holiday with us during the summer months. I think especially of Sally and Richard Lister, who came on several occasions after Richard had sold his farm in Devon. Richard had been a life-long friend of David's and Sally was a very dear friend from St Thomas' days. Richard, with his energy and exuberance, was a great help to Chris…there was always plenty to do in terms of house and garden maintenance. Dear Sally, always a lovely companion as well as a warm and generous person, is the first friend we would call on in times of trouble. They were a wonderful and generous support to both Chris and me later on, when Chris was laid low with Parkinson's; a warmth and generosity we will never be able to repay. They liked to sit and paint together, views from the house and of the house itself, and never needed to be entertained!

Another family who were frequent summer visitors to the Dordogne were Chris' younger brother, John, with his wife Lydia and their two children, Luke and Ruth. It was lovely for me to get to know John and Lydia and their splendid and gifted children. Perhaps for Chris, also, it was an opportunity to get to know John better as an adult. Because their births were separated by the war, they had never been close as children and by the time that John was old enough to be a companion, Chris had left home to join the Merchant Navy. We were also able to hear news from them of Chris' mother, Ruth, who had spent her final years living in a separate flat in their large house in Warrington. She was a gentle and lovely person as well as being an important person in Chris' life. They had spent the war years alone together, throughout the London blitz, while Chris' father, Bernard, was trawling the Caribbean for mines as a naval captain. She had been Chris' whole world, and I suspect that during those lonely and difficult years, he was also her's. Sadly, I never met Chris' father, who had died before we were married, during our sailing holiday in Turkey.

John had retired early from his teaching post in a small public school near to their home in Warrington. He enjoyed spending his days writing, making things in woodwork as well as flying light aircraft; he is especially gifted as a short story writer while Lydia is a very fine artist. We had lovely times together and Chris was impressed and delighted by his niece and nephew

In 2001 I took a six-month sabbatical from work to write a biography of my father, which was something I had been meaning to do since my 20s. Now, at the age of 64, I was finally ready to devote time to it.

While we were still living in London I had approached the editor of Routledge, the publishing company that had previously published my father's book, *Mythology of the Soul.* At the time the Editor was contemplating a new edition. He took me out to lunch and told me he would very much like to publish my biography. While we were eating, he rather coyly put his hand into his breast pocket and pulled out a frayed letter in Jung's handwriting. It was, he said, his most precious possession. Anything connected to Jung was for him beyond price, so a book about the man who had worked most closely with Jung was therefore of great interest to him. However, some weeks later he contacted me to say that it wouldn't be possible after all. The company had a new policy, which stated that they could not publish a book without a guarantee that it would be a commercial success. This was a disappointment to us both.

Some months later, however, Chris and I were in Zurich at the Jung Institute, in order to attend a lecture given by Sir Laurens van der Post to the students. Chris had work in Zurich that was connected with his job at the Swiss Bank Corporation. The title of Van der Post's talk was *Jung in Africa.* It was an hour's lecture, given without a note, by a man who was then about 83 years old. He managed to hold his audience spellbound throughout and was, indeed, the most brilliant storyteller.

After his lecture I went to congratulate him and to tell him who I was. He had known my father and my godmother, Midiboo, was of course, his mother-in-law. He greeted me most warmly, calling me by my nickname, Dinny, and told me that if ever I needed a recommendation for Jungian training, he would be happy to sponsor me. I told him that I was looking for a publisher for my book, which by then was well under way, and he immediately introduced me to Robert Hinshaw, who was the publisher of Jungian books in Zurich. Bob showed interest and after reading my synopsis was very happy to agree to publish the book. As we worked together over the book Bob was both supportive and encouraging and this was the beginning of a warm and exciting collaboration.

So, with the question of a publisher resolved, it was time to get down to the writing in earnest. Chris and I drove down to Le Mespoul in early June, 2001, and stayed until September. I took with me all the relevant documents, which included my father's journals, beginning in 1920, when he started his analysis with Jung, and continuing until his death in 1943. I also had all the letters he had written to my mother when he was still working as Jung's assistant in Zurich - particularly his love letters to her in the 30's - and his correspondence over the years with Jung himself. It was enough material to be getting on with.

Much had already been published about the early part of my father's life, the bohemian period before WW1. I was able to draw on the published material from his close friends, the composer Sir Arnold Bax (who would become my godfather) and his brother, the writer, Clifford Bax. This circle of people who surrounded the Bax family included the poets Rupert Brooke, Edward Thomas, Frances Cornford and Eleanor Farjeon, the pianist Dame Myra Hess, the writers, Clifford Bax, D.H.Lawrence and David Garnet and the artists Jacques and Gwen Raverat.

In many of the accounts of those giddy years when all Victorian restraints and conventions were being discarded, my father's name crops up as the young doctor who could outshine his peers in terms of charm and physical prowess. He was able to delight the ladies and also keep up with the intellectual climate of his gifted bohemian companions.

In addition, I had a brief memoir given to me by my

half-sister Chloe. It had been written by her mother, Rosalind Thorneycroft, my father's first wife, with the title, *Time Which Spaces Us Apart.* It gives a vivid impression of my father's dynamic and magnetic personality at this stage in his life and of his energy, charisma and universal popularity with both men and women. He almost seemed to be lionised by this brilliant group of intellectuals.

So there was no shortage of material and I had nearly all of it with me in France. Chris and I had very structured days. We arose at 6.00 am, when the mist still lay low in the valley and I enjoyed a swim before breakfast. Then Chris and I began work together; he was building a kitchen and I would go to the little house where I had all my research documents, a desk and my computer. We worked each day until 1.00 pm, with a break for coffee, and in the afternoons we lay together in hammocks attached to the two fig trees in the orchard and read and dozed in the sun. Then the serious business of the day began: deciding where, in this gastronomic heaven of the Dordogne, to have our evening meal. At the time, one could still enjoy an haute cuisine meal with wine for as little as 15 euros each.

The days slipped by and both the book and the kitchen grew. By the time we were ready to go home in September, the kitchen was complete and the book was well under way. It was a very lovely way to spend one's life, in an environment entirely free from all stress. These were wonderful days and we returned home with some reluctance. I had a feeling that being a writer would be a fine way to live one's life: living in a beautiful place in the sun, writing for, perhaps, six hours, and then having the rest of the day to play. But of course, I know it isn't always like that. In reality there are difficulties to grapple with, such as unsupportive publishers and editors and writer's block!

However, while we were enjoying the tranquillity and solitude of the lovely Dordogne, things were not as peaceful in the rest of the world; that September the horrors of 9/11 occurred. We received no news in the Dordogne. It was only because, Matthew, 'phoned us at the time of the attack that we knew anything about it. We were particularly concerned because Chris' youngest son, Andrew, was living in New York City at the time.

During our absence, some friends of Anne and Willy Charlton, John and Victoria Jolliffe, came to live in our house. They were planning to move from their home in Somerset and needed to house-hunt in Northumberland. Our home was a convenient place for them and it was good to know that the house was inhabited and cared for. My sabbatical lasted another three months after our return home; during that time I was able to complete the book and prepare it for publication. The book was expertly edited by Nicola and the final edition was given another intensely thorough edit by my nephew, Jonathan Baynes, who left every page blackened with corrections. The result was a text almost free from errors.

At the book launch at our home, in the autumn of that year, all our closest friends were invited and my friend, Anne Charlton, gave such a warm and lovely introduction for the book as well as a glowing account of the authoress herself! I could hardly see myself reflected there but was warmed and grateful to her for such wonderful affirmation. Anne has become one of my closest friends. She also has trained as a psychotherapist and as a group therapist and we have, over the years, helped one another through our hopes and fears, family troubles and bereavements. Her wisdom and warm friendship have been a source of comfort and support through some difficult times. We arranged to meet one another once a month, alternating between our homes. We each have one hour to speak of ourselves and then we have a walk across country. At her moorland home in West Woodburn, we walk along the mowed paths along the River Rede and over their farmland, and at my home, we walk along muddy paths in our woodland and across the fields.

We then return home for a light lunch. These have been treasured times when we can share our inner most thoughts and experiences without the fear of indiscretions! Anne is a wise and wonderfully positive person who remains fully available to others and to life in spite of the many losses throughout her life…most recently the loss of her beloved daughter, Tessa. I shall always be grateful for the warmth and wisdom of her friendship.

My book was well received in the Jungian world, as well as by the Jung family. It isn't a book that has wide appeal but it does, perhaps, provide a unique and very personal view of Jung himself. He was my father's teacher, guide and friend for 23 years and my father had been his assistant in Zurich for several of those years. It is possible I also needed to write the book to get to know my father; not through the eyes of a small child but as an adult, no longer influenced by my mother's rather biased view of him.

Since my own training as a Jungian-based psychotherapist, it had become more important to get to know him as a man and to discover his impact in the world of Jungian psychology, rather than to know him simply as a father. I also wanted the world to recognize what he had achieved. His successor, Michael Fordham, had managed almost to delete my father from the history of Jungian psychology in the U.K., forgetting that my father was, indeed, the pioneer and the first person to establish a Jungian school, as well as the Jungian Club, in London. The Club is still flourishing.

Chapter 18

Parkinson's Disease

On New Years day, 1993, we decide to give a reel party, together with the Trevelyan family, in the village hall in Stamfordham. It was Anna's idea to have a shared New Year's party with Scottish reels and a buffet supper. There was a piper, a violinist and a caller. Chris and I had often danced reels together and he was an exceptionally good dancer. On this occasion, however, he was all over the place. The caller would say 'Turn to the right!' and Chris would turn to the left, then, 'Spin your partner!' and Chris would have difficulty remaining upright. People were laughing at him, presuming that he was drunk.

Later, when the party was over and we were in bed together, he told me that he wasn't, in fact, drunk and that for some time he had been experiencing problems, but hadn't wanted to worry me with them. He had been having difficulty with balance and a problem also with shaving and writing. He said at once, 'I wonder whether I have Parkinson's disease.' I was considering the possibility of a brain tumour, so Parkinson's seemed like the lesser of two evils.

The following day I was on the telephone to Andrew Henderson, who told me that Chris should have the symptoms checked without delay. Andrew arranged for him to see David Bates, an associate of his and the top neurologist in Newcastle. David Bates saw Chris that very afternoon, at the end of his working day. Chris enumerated his various problems and finally David Bates said, 'You have just told me all the symptoms of Parkinson's disease.' He was in a hurry to leave, to meet his son from school, and omitted to tell Chris anything at all about the disease, its treatment and what he might expect in the long term.

This diagnosis was a mighty blow for the whole family. Chris had always been well: the strong one, the one who seemed never to tire. He hadn't taken a single day off work throughout the years of bringing up his children. It seemed inconceivable that he should be unwell. But when we began to reflect, we could see that these problems had been around for as long as Chris and I had known each other. Very early in our friendship, he had come over one day for lunch and I had suggested a bike ride. We still had David's bike in the garage but to my great surprise, Chris was unable to ride it; he found he couldn't balance so we had to abandon bikes and walk instead. This seemed strange for a fit and athletic man. During another walk, I jumped over a small stream. Chris came after me and instead of reaching the bank on the far side he landed in the stream. I remember being puzzled by this, but they were just isolated events. With hindsight, it seemed to us that this had been creeping up on him for some time and perhaps even *before* we met.

We were appalled by the news. The day after our party - a day of ice and snow - we went for a long walk together to the pretty village of Blanchland. Chris drove our Volvo station wagon home. Ice had started to form on the roads as the daytime temperature dropped and Chris went too fast round the A69, Corbridge roundabout. The car went out of control and landed upside down on the bank.

I had a cut or two and we both suffered from shock but were not seriously hurt. We were taken to A&E and then returned home by taxi; the car was a write-off. Things were clearly not right! After the official diagnosis arrived from Dr Burn we both felt we needed a holiday and my dear sister in law, Jill Walker and her husband Jimmy, suggested we go out to Barbados to stay with them and forget our worries for a time. Which is what we did. The following week we were on a 'plane and received a wonderfully warm welcome from the Walker family.

We had the holiday of a lifetime. We stayed in the

bungalow next to Jill and Jimmy's plantation house and had our own car. It was two weeks of paradise. We were able to put on hold the whole new prospect of a life-sentence. Having nursed my mother with Parkinsons I had no illusion as to how difficult it could be. We spent most of those weeks on the beach, swimming and snorkelling and basking in the beautiful Caribbean sun. The Walkers were endlessly hospitable and we spent happy evenings together with Jill and Jimmy's daughter and son-in-law, Sue and Chris, and their daughter, Holly, who was just 18 months old.

Chris had been working for the Tyne and Wear Development Corporation for a little over a year. He was enjoying the challenge and variety involved in assessing small businesses in the North East for their viability as well as their suitability for receiving a government grant. The TWDC was a quango that had been set up by Michael Heseltine to promote business initiatives in the northern region, an area of Britain that had lagged behind the rest of the UK economically. His job entailed visiting the proposed site and the new manager and requesting a business plan. On the strength of the plan, it was then decided whether or not the business would be viable financially. There was variety and challenge in the job and Chris met some interesting and enterprising people.

Chris had been working for Tyne and Wear Development Corporation for five years when he finally told them of his diagnosis of Parkinson's. The quango was about to be shut down anyway, so it seemed a good moment to take early retirement on health grounds.

Normal life continued, with little physical impairment, for about ten years. The medication worked well and Chris enjoyed days of leisure for the first time in his life. These were good years for us both. Chris was active in the house and garden; he enjoyed making things, maintaining our home and using his creative abilities in so many ways. He drove several times a year to the Dordogne and loved being there on his own. I went with him when I could take a holiday from work. It was as though Parkinson's disease had given him permission to do the things he really enjoyed. When the medication was working, he was fully mobile and there was little effect on him either mentally or physically.

* * *

Learning to live together and to become one family took a number of years, and we had some hiccups along the way. At first the boys were delighted to have three pretty sisters and the girls' longing for brothers was in some way fulfilled by Chris's sons. There was an especially strong friendship between Matthew and Cathy, and later, in London, between Cathy and Andrew. The Jansen family had hardly interacted with Nicola because she had already left home when Chris and I married. However, there were also moments of resentment among the sisters when, from time to time, their home was taken over by four large young men and their friends. The boys were similarly quite possessive of their London home and resented the many hours the girls spent in the shower and the fact that they used too much loo paper! But these were teething problems and on the whole, there was little tension between them.

Chris and I also had our difficulties and we had to discover how to be together. Chris had brought up his boys on his own and resented any kind of suggestion or interference from me, so I soon learned to only give help or advice when asked. The boys knew that Chris was touchy about my involvement with them and would sometimes come to me with a problem, saying, 'Please, Diana, would you put on your counsellor's hat?' which simply meant, 'Don't tell Dad.'

Chris could also be critical. He had been used to reprimanding his sons publicly and began to do this with me as well. At a dinner party, I might make a remark and Chris would say, in front of everyone, 'What on earth was the relevance of that?' I found this deeply embarrassing. He criticised me in the same way that he would check his sons: a running commentary of little denigrating remarks. In general, they weren't in themselves anything important, but collectively they had an undermining effect.

It happened one day when we were together in the Dordogne. Chris had been speaking in French with our neighbour, Robert, learning about the five years he spent in a prisoner of war camp in Germany during WWII. I had been reading beside the pool. I had promised to treat Chris to supper at a local restaurant that evening. After his conversation with Robert, Chris joined me by the pool and he made several critical and denigrating remarks. I didn't say anything but was feeling a little unhappy as we set out for the restaurant.

We had just begun on the hors d'oeuvres when he made another remark, possibly not really offensive, but his negative comments had continued all day and like water dripping on a stone they had a cumulative effect. I snapped. I can't say exactly what happened or why, but I began to cry, uncontrollably, there in the restaurant, something I had never done in my life before.

Chris was embarrassed and told me to go to the loo and pull myself together. I tried to stop crying: wiped my eyes, blew my nose but it was as though a dam had burst. Finally, we had to pay the bill without having eaten anything, leave the restaurant and still I couldn't stop crying! By this time Chris was seriously concerned. I told him not to worry; that it was only tears. But I struggled to stop crying the whole evening. Neither of us ever understood what had happened that night but Chris never made denigrating remarks again. He did criticise, but no longer with the continual undermining remarks that married people so frequently level at one another. I believe until that evening Chris was entirely unaware that he was doing it.

So, little by little we became more accepting of one another. I learned to be more aware of Chris' needs; the needs of someone who had had no adult to consider him since the death of Veronica. Chris learned to express, in words, how he was feeling. At the beginning he considered that emotion and any *show* of feeling was off limits. And yet, he was a profoundly sensitive and deep-feeling person. If I ever pointed out to him that something he said or did was hurtful or tactless he would never make the same mistake again. With the advent of Parkinsons, he no longer had such a firm grip on himself and he became a much warmer and more 'feeling' person. His sons noticed this also. It was as though he could now relax and just be himself. It also gave him an excuse to sit back a little, something he had, in the past, never had the time to do.

When David and I bought our house in Dalton in 1970, the half acre of garden that had once been the original vegetable garden had planning permission. During the 30 years that it was our home we renewed the planning permission every three years. The request always had to be publicised at the time of application, in case there were any objections. Someone would turn up every time this occurred and ask if they could buy the land from us. It was a valuable plot because the only permission that could be granted was for 'in-filling' and ours was the last available plot in Dalton.

Chris and I were beginning to find The Cottage and its large garden too much for us so we considered the possibility of building a smaller house on the building plot. We applied for planning permission for a Swedish Scandia Haus, timber-framed, but clad in stone, which would be in keeping with the rest of the village. We submitted our plans for a house that looked, from the outside, like a typical Northumbrian sandstone house. Our plans were accepted. At first Chris wondered whether he would still have the energy and ability to mastermind such a project, but he finally decided to bite the bullet. He drew up the plans for the interior of the house, which roughly conformed to the Scandia Haus model, but he added onto the Swedish design a separate annex with loo and a consulting room and its own separate front door, so patients wouldn't need to come through the house.

When the foundations were dug, an archaeologist had to be present in case any Roman remains might be lying beneath our garden; fortunately, nothing was found. The timber frame then arrived in three large containers and was assembled in six days. After that, it took another six months for the stonemasons, Peter Spratt and his son Jason, to complete the stone cladding. The workmen used our workshop at The Cottage for their tea breaks and we noticed how the stone masons were certainly top of the pecking order, in relation to the joiners, slaters, the plumber, electricians and decorators. They always had first claim on the facilities!

Chris oversaw the project and was busy with the men from morning to night, fixing curtain rails and doing whatever jobs he was still able to manage. He loved working alongside the builders and acting as foreman. It took a year to complete the house; Chris had made all the decisions about the layout and took delight in designing most of the interior, particularly the staircase, the banister and the beautiful oak front door. It was something that consumed him totally, involving all his creative and practical gifts. It amazed me how skilled he was and how well he could envision what the plan would look when it was finally realized in three dimensions.

The house he created is compact. On the ground floor there are three main south-facing rooms, these all lead into a large conservatory at the back, which stretches along the entire northern aspect of the house and has a grand view of the garden. A wide lawn leads to the magnificent sycamore tree that once stood in our old garden, with a shrubbery bordering the lawn on either side. In the hedge at the end of the garden a small archway has been cut to allow a view up to the field and beyond to where the sheep are grazing. As it is a Swedish house it has sub-zero standard insulation in all the walls, so the Aga gives off enough heat to warm the entire house. In addition, the house was designed for wheelchair access, although at the time Chris did not yet need one, so it was the ideal house for the next stage in our life. It was almost as though in building this house Chris had foreseen everything.

It was autumn when the house was finally ready for us to move in. The preceding weeks had been fraught with difficulty because The Cottage was sold and we needed to move out on a certain date. Our house was still not structurally complete two weeks before this date. We made it just in time, but Chris was ill, exhausted and suffering from severe sciatica. He was too unwell to take an active part in the move but watched, bewildered, as the contents of The Cottage were transferred to the new house. I moved most of the contents myself - apart from the heavy furniture - using the tractor mower and trailer. It is astonishing how much stuff can accumulate when you have two lofts and five out-houses. It was a long job! Poor Chris found it all too much; the Parkinson's took a drastic nose-dive, partly, perhaps, on account of the move, but mostly due to the pain from his sciatica. So, he was now wheelchair- bound.

I finally managed to persuade the surgeon to operate, although he considered Chris' condition to be more of a medical than a surgical problem. I had to turn on the histrionics to some extent to persuade him to go ahead. So, two weeks after our move Chris was in the Newcastle General Hospital under-going surgery for decompression of the spine. The operation was totally successful. Two days after the operation Chris could walk again and there was a dramatic improvement in the Parkinson's. He was allowed to come home when he could manage the stairs. Within a week Matthew and I went to collect him. He was able to walk the two hundred yards down Westgate Road to have a grand lunch at the Pinocchio Italian restaurant, having eaten almost nothing of the revolting hospital food.

During the next few years the Parkinson's gradually worsened. It was imperceptible at first. We were still able to go to the Dordogne two or three times a year and Chris could enjoy maintaining his new home and making things in the workshop. He was enormously proud of the house he had created and just being in it gave him great pleasure. In all the homes he had lived in with his sons, he had never made any real impression on them, leaving the decoration and furnishings as he had found them. But he had created everything in our new home: the design and layout, the furnishings and colour schemes. From the moment it was built it felt like a lovely place to be: the sun pours in, the rooms are spacious and warm and from every window there are lovely views of the garden and the fields beyond. To have created such a house when he was already suffering from advanced Parkinson's disease is truly remarkable. Our home is a most wonderful tribute to him.

After we had lived in the house for about five years things became suddenly much worse. Chris' balance had been deteriorating; when he was over-dosed on Madopar (the drug that replaces the Dopamine), he suffered from involuntary movements, known as dyskinesia. If he tried to walk when he had dyskinesia he tended to fall. This might happen several times every day. He even fell down the stairs, from top to bottom, twice, but miraculously he never hurt himself. He seemed to learn to fall like a cat and was able to remain totally relaxed.

But then one evening, we were sitting watching the television; he got up suddenly to fetch something and fell, banging his head on the corner of the Aga. Blood spurted out, copiously, and he became extremely alarmed. It was, in reality, only a small cut which didn't require stitches, just a little mopping up. The bleeding soon stopped. But he was frightened by this episode and didn't really want to walk again, so the accident marked the beginning of his confinement to a wheelchair. Now, perhaps for the first time, he began to *feel* like a disabled person.

We went on two holidays together to hotels designed for the disabled, with all the necessary equipment and as much help as we required. One was in Crete and the other in Tuscany. Both were lovely holidays where we were able to relax and feel real pleasure that we could still come away together to beautiful places and enjoy a honeymoon feeling all over again. Chris was a lovely companion. He never complained and his sense of humour remained intact to the very end. He wanted to remain self-sufficient and no matter how much he needed *physical* assistance, he retained an independence of spirit. Someone once commented that through all his disabilities he maintained an inner dignity, which is true.

We took a final holiday at the hotel in the Dordogne where both Matthew and Michele and Cathy and Roman had celebrated their weddings. (We had to sell our Dordogne properties when Chris began to need a wheelchair which was, indeed, a sad time!) This last holiday was our farewell to that lovely part of France and to our friends there - the Treays, the Gortons, the Fieldens and our French friend, Brigitte La Croix. In Le Salvetat we had a downstairs room, everywhere was wheel chair friendly, the pool entirely accessible and the cuisine, superb. The sun shone, and we felt again the sense of unlimited time and the healing effect of the gentle, rolling countryside with its woods and valleys and its wealth of wild flowers.

At the time we didn't know that it was to be our last holiday together.

Nicola and Bill on their wedding day

Cathy and Roman at their wedding in the Dordogne

Grandchildren

For both Chris and me, what has brought us greatest joy as we have grown older, is our grandchildren. Altogether we have 15. Each of my daughters has two children and Chris' sons have the other 9. We haven't kept up with all of them as some of the marriages have come apart and we have lost touch with two of the older children.

For me, these children are a wonderful gift - the gift of the future and each one, in his or her own way, is totally splendid. In the compass of this book it would take too long to give a detailed description of each of them. Also, this memoir is being written principally about the time before they were born, so they will have a glimpse into the past. They already know about their own lives!

I have had more enjoyment from my grandchildren than I can possibly express; each one in his or her individual way is uniquely special. I remember times spent with Anna and Tessa when they were tiny. They stayed with us each year while Nicola and Bill took an annual honeymoon at Whitsun. I think of one magical day spent in the sun while I sat and watched them play, absorbed in their game of mothers and fathers. Jock, our beloved golden Labrador, lent them his kennel for the day. This was their house and his straw their bed and a bucket of water became their pool. This game absorbed them for hours together, with Anna as the Mummy and Tessa as her baby. And another memorable time was in the Dordogne, after the wedding of Cathy and Roman. I had given Tessa a wedding dress for her third birthday present. For the rest of the holiday they re-enacted the wedding together, taking it in turns to be the bride and solemnly walking up the grassy aisle together and then exchanging a kiss. Now, Anna's beautiful singing moves me to tears and Tessa is already a budding Michael Angelo, with her exquisite drawings.

I remember Helena's Joe, an enchanting small boy of

three, holding my hand as we walked up the hill to feed the pigs in the Dordogne. The farm lay below us and early morning mist obscured the valley. I think of his delight in this whole adventure and my thought, 'Perhaps I will never be this happy again!' There were early morning visits at their home in Norfolk, when Joe and Rosy would come into my bed, to hear stories…and to tell me 'secrets'! Such precious times. And later, there were long afternoons playing board games, with Joe always a jump or two ahead, especially with Monopoly. I never won a single game, and Rosie's encouragement when I was losing disastrously yet again; 'Believe in yourself Granny, believe in yourself!' And I think of Rosy, so articulate and aware of everything and everyone so early in life; dictating a story to me about fairies when she was no more than four or five, with an extraordinary fluency. And walking together to her school, her hand in mine, her blond hair like spun gold glowing in the sunshine.

Helena has had a hard time as a single Mum. She and Rex separated before Rosy was born. She has been a wonderful mother and is also, (working as a clinical psychologist), the sole bread-winner; a tall order! I remember a particular occasion when I was staying with them. It had been a busy day with Rosy's third birthday party. That evening, Joe was being demanding and awkward and tearful. Eventually, Helena stopped what she was doing, and said to him; 'I think you are upset because it is Rosy's birthday and she has had all the attention today.' Immediately, Joe stopped crying, and simply said 'yes'. She had given a name to his feelings and that was enough. They went upstairs and had a together time while Helena talked to him. He came downstairs perfectly happy and serene and came to sit beside me. I said; 'Joe, would you like to play a game?' His reply was; 'Hush Granny, I'm having a quiet time.' If only all life's problems could be solved that easily!

With Fynn I had wonderful times when he was two and

his family lived in Botswana. I think of the daily visits of elephants and baboons through their camp and the view over the savannah of zebras and antelope and of hippos and crocs wallowing in the mud: this was Fynn's daily environment. Among the trees and long grasses surrounding their camp we played hide-and-seek with Easter eggs; he was delighted and excited every time he found one. He was already an expert at identifying animal spoors and elephant poo! Then, little Gemma, who has a wonderful temperament; she seems to glow and just to see her makes you feel better. I remember a long walk alone with her in Anstruther, (near St Andrews), when Cathy and Roman were living in Scotland. Fynn was already at school, and Gemma was just three. We were looking for wild flowers and naming the one's we knew. Already, even at that early age, she showed an astonishing awareness as well as interest, in the world around her. She was so little but already, somehow, so wise. She was attending her first nursey school in Scotland while I was staying and on her first day the teacher asked her name. She replied: 'Gemma Wicked.' She couldn't yet pronounce her surname, 'Wittig'!

Such precious moments. And there are many others that I will always treasure. I see in them traces of David, (in Fynn); of Mickey, (in Joe), and of my mother, (in Rosy). So, in these beautiful children, the past and the future come together. Anna and Tessa also have such strong characteristics of their parents. Once when Anna was looking at a photo of two-year old Nicola together with David, she asked, 'Who am I talking to in that picture Mummy?' At that early stage they were amazingly alike. She also has Nicola's passionate temperament and determination. Tessa is more like her Dad, with her calm and gentle nature and her considerable artistic gifts. Perhaps Gemma, with her sunny temperament and ability to get on with everyone, is very much like *her* Mum, also!

For Chris, also, his grandchildren were his greatest

delight as they too represented the future, which he had worked so hard for in bringing up his children single-handedly. They are the legacy of his beautiful young wife who tragically lost her life at the young age of 29. All Chris's grandchildren are exceptionally able; his six granddaughters are all beautiful, while his three grandsons each excel in their own way. In these children we have both been blessed. After having had so many bereavements in our lives, the grandchildren represent both life and the future.

Chapter 19

Final Chapter

In the autumn of 2015, life became rapidly more difficult. The sciatic pain Chris had suffered 12 years previously, returned, and treatment for this was delayed because the surgeon was away. The Parkinson's disease deteriorated again and Chris was physically unable to do very much; he needed help with virtually everything. Vera Linney, who had been helping us for ten years, making it possible for us to lead almost normal lives and allowing me to work and pursue my interests, was a tower of strength at this time. Vera, for so many years, had been our guardian angel. She came to help us every day and as she lived only 3 minutes away, she offered to be 'on call' if I went out. How very different those years, as Chris' condition gradually deteriorated, would have been, without her wonderful spirit, expertise, energy and devotion to Chris. It is impossible to express what she has meant to us all, but most especially, to Chris.

It was a few days before Christmas; everything was ready and Justin and Matthew and their families were going to be with us over the holiday period. We decided to have a few neighbours in for drinks on the evening of the 22nd December. We had a merry evening; Chris supplied champagne and nibbles and sat on the sofa between our neighbours, Ross (Vera's son) and his partner, Louise. Chris was on great form, cracking jokes and making everyone laugh. After drinks, Chris and I had a light supper and then I sat beside him to watch the news before we went to bed.

With the help of the hoist I lifted Chris from his armchair and wheeled him to the stair lift. Then, again with the help of the hoist, I lifted him onto the stair lift. I returned to the kitchen to turn off the lights. As I did so I heard a terrible crash. Chris had fallen from the stair lift and was unconscious on the floor. I took his pulse: nothing. He had stopped breathing. I carried out CPR and mouth-to-mouth resuscitation, without success.

I 'phoned 999. Then I 'phoned Vera's son, Ross. He came at once (from his cottage just two houses away), and took over the CPR from me, pumping with all his strength until Chris started breathing again. Within eight minutes the first ambulance had arrived, followed shortly afterwards by a second. Chris had a weak pulse and his breathing was becoming more normal. The second ambulance was ready to drive him to the RVI. Ross suggested I prepare a bag in case I needed to stay overnight. I assembled a few things and travelled in the ambulance, sitting next to the driver, with the siren and the blue lights flashing. The ambulance man said, 'If your husband survives, it will be your friend who has saved his life.'

When we arrived at the RVI Chris was taken straight into theatre. He was alive, just, but I was told, 'We can keep him alive, but he will have no quality of life and his brain will be affected.' He had suffered a severe pulmonary embolism.

The medics suggested that I ring his sons and that we make this decision together. I was able to reach Justin on his mobile 'phone, (by now it was well past midnight). He managed to arouse Matthew and they both arrived within half an hour. We talked and decided that Chris would not enjoy a half-life. It was recommended that the ventilator should be turned off. The three of us were together, feeling dazed and confused but knowing that for Chris, this *was* the right decision. It was early morning. Matthew managed to wake Simon in Mallorca, (thank goodness for mobile 'phones and for the fact that many people keep them on at night!), and he then got hold of Andrew in Los Angeles.

We stood next to Chris and watched while the medics

switched off the ventilator. His blood pressure gradually dropped until it reached zero. Then we knew that the end had come. We were in contact with Simon and Andrew, so it was as if his whole family was there, at his bedside. Andrew texted Matthew to say, 'I haven't been a very good son.' (Chris had had almost no contact with him during the previous seven years). However, Matthew replied, 'You have been a wonderful son and Daddy was so proud of you,' which was true. From having been Chris's greatest cause for concern and source of anxiety, Andrew had become stunningly successful in his field and had just recently been awarded an Emmy for his work as a cameraman.

Chris died at 3.00 am. We were asked if he would have liked a Catholic priest to administer the last rites. We all agreed he would have welcomed it. Within half an hour the priest was with us. His first words, on seeing Chris lying so still on the stretcher were, 'What a noble face.' He did indeed look very peaceful and I felt that he had been spared any more suffering, as well as the degradation that would have been inevitable with further helplessness. The priest administered the last rites and then asked us about Chris.

Justin and Matthew told him what an amazing dad he had been, sacrificing everything for his sons and how he had sent the four of them to school at Ampleforth. The priest commented that he must have been very well off to afford the school fees for four boys. Matthew replied, 'On the contrary, the little he had, he spent on his sons.' Chris possessed a beaten-up old Vauxhall car during the whole of their childhood and lived his life with the greatest simplicity. 'He didn't have a materialistic bone in his body,' Matthew told the priest.

It felt as though this little ceremony in the early hours of December 23rd was a celebration of Chris, his courage and his amazing achievements with regard to his children. He had an unquenchable faith in life which he has passed on to his children. His four sons were his pride and joy and came before everything. It never occurred to him that he had achieved anything out of the ordinary. His great ambition would have been to obtain military honours but his life as a military man was cut short. In terms of courage and the qualities of enduring love and fortitude, his achievement was, perhaps, akin to a Military Cross. Few men could have achieved what he did and with so little sense of his own self-sacrifice.

The three of us arrived home at 6.00 am; Matthew carried on to Acomb as he had work the following day. I realized that I had a patient arriving at 10.00 am, as I had been unable to reach her to cancel the session. It was a short night but somehow I managed to put aside the events of the night in order to listen to someone else's troubles. This was possibly something that I learned to do when I was nursing - to switch into professional mode so that one's own concerns did not interfere with the ability to attend to another person's needs.

The next days were so busy there was no time to think or to grieve. As everything would be closed until after New Year, it was necessary to register the death and to deal with all the practical concerns in the two days left before Christmas. Matthew and I went to the registry office the following day, to register Chris's death. We informed the Parkinson's disease department at the RVI where the two Parkinson's nurses, Oona and Trish, had looked after Chris for 20 years with care and treatment that was second to none. Finally, we informed our local G.P. practice.

There was no time to think about how my life would change. Justin and Matthew arrived with their families to celebrate Christmas, just as we had planned. It all passed as though in a dream. How strange it was to discover the parcel that Chris had prepared for me: a beautiful skirt, which was a perfect fit and so elegantly wrapped. But as he wasn't there to thank, it felt extraordinarily poignant.

It wasn't until after Christmas, when everyone had left and the rest of the world was busy celebrating with their families that I really began to feel the impact of Chris's death. Never in my life had I felt so alone. I knew that we had almost reached the stage when we wouldn't be able to manage without respite care and I knew that was something Chris would never have countenanced. In some ways, and with my 80th birthday not far away, we had perhaps almost reached the end of the road.

But grief is not rational. For me it felt as though *my* world had come to an end. I couldn't imagine a life after Chris. Caring for him had taken up the greater part of my life for many years, particularly towards the end. Now, suddenly, there was nothing. Facing 'nothingness' is an altogether terrifying prospect. I had other interests and occupations and I was still working a little, but for many years my whole life had revolved around Chris and his needs. To begin with it felt as if I no longer had anything to live for.

I wrote of this bleakness, 'Caught in the spiral of grief. No comfort. Just a pain that seems to be eternal, everlasting and universal.' A feeling of such utter despair that at times felt like a bottomless pit. But then, there *is* a sense of life returning, like a hint of sun coming through the clouds. I wrote of, 'Moments of intense joy – this morning, banks of flame-coloured, low cloud and then the sun, an orange orb, breaking through. Dark shapes of spiky branches, a sparrow hawk, or perhaps a buzzard, roosting, taking flight with slow-wing beat then gliding, upwards and out of sight.' It was just the beginning of a feeling that there could be life after Chris.

Sometime later I wrote a poem, which seemed to give expression to the connection between us:

I pick up the phone
I hear your voice
crisp and clear.

I want to tell you
I have varnished
the oak front door.
Can you hear me?

A pungent smell;
don't touch it,
the varnish is wet.
It is your door.

Our door; the door
that opened between us;
between your loss and mine.
The seven children became ours.

I look inside the door,
noone there,
just your voice:

'This is Chris and Diana's phone,
please leave a message after the tone.'
I'm leaving a message;
I have lost you…

It's the word 'forever'
which grows, mushroom like.
Loss is a hole in the universe
into which all the known world

disappears. But I know
Why the moon tonight has
become so big and so round.
It's your face, looking down.

And so, I was to discover that life *does* go on. A new sense
of living for life's sake and not in relation to another person

gradually began to develop. It is a kind of freedom knowing that there is a raison d'être that doesn't have to involve another person. Is it liberation from having to be what another is expecting or needing? Such a thing had never happened to me before. I have always experienced my aliveness and my sense of personal identity in relation to someone else. Now, there *is* no 'someone else'. Who am I in relation to *me*? That is still a very novel concept!

Chapter 20

Life After Death

It is nearly three years now since Chris's death and I have passed the big 80 year landmark, with many celebrations. Life is full and there have been some wonderful times, with opportunities to travel and visit far-flung family and friends.

I spent memorable weeks being entertained and celebrated by my brother Christopher's eight children and all the grandchildren, (25 in all, together with 15 great grandchildren), in New Zealand. My visits to everyone were organized by Christopher's eldest daughter, Gillian, who has become a wise and wonderful friend. The visit began with lovely and gentle days with Gillian and Adrian in their beautiful home on Waiheke Island, swimming in the sea below their house, sailing and even playing tennis, and also enjoying listening to Gillian as she played her violin in a local children's production. We visited together their holiday home on Lake Tekapo and made trips to tourist sites; the Waitomo Glow Worm Caves and the Otorohanga Kiwi House. I paid visits to Vinnie, Len and Anthony; to Nancy and her family and to Hugo on the eve of the wedding of his lovely daughter. In what had been the family home, Cae Crin, and is now owned by Len, (the original Black Rider in the *Lord of the Rings*), I was able to have time with Lorna, who was living nearby in a residential home and also with Rob and Hilary. I felt embraced by all the family and welcomed with heart-warming generosity and had such a strong sense of belonging to this wonderful and vibrant family. I realized, also, that I probably wouldn't have a chance to see my sister- in –law, Lorna, again, who was beginning to feel frail, having passed her 90th birthday.

Returning home again after the trip of a life time, I

become more used to being alone and no longer wake each morning with a sense of foreboding in relation to the coming day. Once more there is a sense of life as an adventure and I still experience the excitement of what may happen in the future. The past is a fait accompli but the future still holds surprises and unknown possibilities. I would like to continue to live as full a life as possible and would like to be able to welcome death when my time comes.

I no longer yearn to share my life with anyone and yet derive so much enjoyment and enrichment from the company of my lovely family and my many friends. Life has been rich and rewarding and, although there have been losses and deep sadness, I would not have had it any other way.

Epilogue

Our Families

I haven't yet mentioned all the various members of our combined families. So many lives have now become a part of our daily world. It is difficult to paint a life history of each one; some of our children have had more impact on our lives than others. Many people speak endlessly about their children and their successes and exploits. Chris was very economical when people asked about his children. He could summarize the whole subject in a couple of sentences. So, when speaking about the individual lives of seven children, there is, indeed, a great danger of becoming a bore!

When we married, Justin had just joined the army and was soon to meet his future wife, Rachel, whose father was the Major General of the Royal Marines. They had a splendid military wedding and their first home was a schloss in Detmold. After a few years Justin was given the option of early retirement, so the couple came to live in Northumberland, where Justin worked for a time with the $15^{th}/19^{th}$ branch of the Territorials. There were tensions in the marriage; soon after the birth of their daughter, Charlotte, they separated. A few years later Justin married Vicky, a neighbour in Bothal. They eventually had two lovely children: Olly, who is now a splendid young man and a professional standard tennis player and Bella, who was the apple of Chris's eye. Chris took great delight in buying Bella her first horse, Sid. She would become a fine horsewoman, as well as being a very lovely girl. They continued to live near to us, first in Bothal and later in

Morpeth, until after Chris's death. Justin has spent the years since his retirement from the Army as a very successful photographer, with a special gift for photographing children. His photographs of all our children and grandchildren hang above the stairs and along the landing; he has captured the essence of each person beautifully. Since the breakdown of his marriage to Vicky, Justin has moved to Thailand and has now found happiness with a young Thai woman called Moon with whom he is creating a new home near to Chiang Mai.

Matthew is a year younger than Justin and is a lawyer. After gaining a degree at Kings, London, in both French and English law, he worked as a banking lawyer with the London firm, Allen and Overy, and was later sent by the company to France where he was able to work as an avocat. He lived a luxurious life in Paris in a beautiful apartment with a view over-looking the golden dome of Les Invalides. He married Michele, who worked as an office manager in a Parisian law firm and they had a splendid wedding in the Dordogne, in what was to become our second home. They had two children, Thomas and Camille, who are both talented and bilingual. Thomas is now at Bristol University studying civil engineering and has become deeply involved in Zen Buddhism. He is a gentle and thoughtful young man; very like his Dad was at the same age. Camille is just 18 and is another exceptionally lovely girl. She has made a considerable name for herself on Instagram as both a model and a person to be admired. She has a following of over 200,000 and already has a career mapped out for her in modelling, if she chooses that life. Like Vicky, Michele already had two children from a previous marriage. Her marriage to Matthew also ran into difficulties and Matthew eventually left Allen and Overy - and Paris - in order to become a legal translator, working from home. He now has a long-term partner, Jo, who is loved by all the family.

Simon is two years younger than Matthew and is the same age as Helena. A very successful property entrepreneur, he made a fortune buying and selling properties in Gateshead and he eventually moved to Mallorca with his lovely wife, Becky. They have three children, Freddy, Lara and Amelia. The family has moved house many times - almost every year - due to the fluctuations in Simon's work: from Mallorca to Newcastle to Northumberland and, for a time, to Malaysia. The children's stability lay in boarding at Ampleforth, where Chris had sent his four sons. They are now all grown-up and doing well in their different careers. Freddy had a particularly strong relationship with Chris and was the grandchild we saw most of when they were small. He has grown into a splendid and very steady young man. He has finished his training in the Merchant Navy and spends most of the year at sea. Lara is another beauty, with the stunning good looks of her mother, Becky. She never possessed much confidence in her academic ability; when she was just a little girl, perched in a tree and reading a book, she looked down at me and said, 'You see, I'm not the sharpest pencil in the box.' True or not, she has been extremely successful and is now running a very profitable kitchen business in Cheltenham. Amelia was a premature baby and was brought home when she weighed only three pounds. Even the premature baby clothes were far too big for her. But she has since made up for this and has a robust enjoyment of life and confidence in herself and her abilities, so her life is never dull! She is an extremely gifted artist and painting had been her passion since she was small.

Andrew is the youngest of Chris's sons. After leaving school he lived with Chris and me in London for a time, together with an Afro-Caribbean girl, Grace, who became his first wife and the mother of his daughter, Paris. He was more of a worry to Chris and had left Ampleforth without passing any exams. Childhood was possibly more difficult for Andrew, who was only 18 months old when his mother died; it was hard for Chris to fulfil the needs of a baby while working full time.

After marrying Grace and making a home with his family in Florida, Andrew was able to buy a steadycam camera - equipment that had only just become available - with inheritance from an aunt. With this he built up a very successful career, on the back of the expertise he had gathered from his photography lessons and camera work at school. He has now filmed at least three American Presidents, as well as a pope. For a time, he also worked as cameraman to David Beckham when Beckham was living in California and he has won an Emmy for a popular film series on American television. The marriage to Grace was short-lived and he is now married to a very beautiful Filipino girl, called Angelica. They live together in Los Angeles.

So the family is scattered, and we keep in contact mainly on WhatsApp. The children drift in and out of our lives and only come together at times of celebration or mourning; the last time was at Chris's funeral.

Each one of our children with the exception of Nicola, has come home to live with us at some point. When Simon and Becky were between homes, they stayed with us, together with their children, Freddy and Lara. Matthew was with us for six months while he was finding his feet after leaving Paris and starting a new life in the UK as a legal translator. When Helena was completing her training as a clinical psychologist she moved home when things became very tough, as did Cathy, after leaving her job in London as a speech therapist at St Thomas', when she was between careers. Andrew was with us for six months, recovering from testicular cancer and finally, Justin came to live with us during the final six months of Chris's life. He was a helpful and reassuring presence at a particularly stressful time. He is now also based here with me, when he is not in the Far East, and lives in the loft apartment of my house. So, there have been many opportunities to get to know each of our children as adults and individuals, rather than as part of a large family.

As for the three Crockford girls, each one is pursuing a career in which they are fully, and on the whole happily and successfully employed. Nicola is married to Bill, (William Sutherland), who holds the Miriam Rothschild Chair in Cambridge for Conservation Biology. She is working for the RSPB as their endangered species agent world-wide, which involves a great deal of travel. She has recently been in China, leading a delegation of Chinese, North Korean and South Korean politicians and naturalists. The meeting was about endangered species, particularly the spoon-billed sandpiper, and was an attempt to save their breeding grounds from industrial development. In spite of the tricky relationship between North and South Korea, this mission has turned out to be entirely successful. She has recently managed to prevail upon the Chinese Government to create the whole of the Yellow Sea as a conservation area. No mean feat, and she has been celebrated by the Chinese government by being made a Friend of Jiangsu Province. So, she and Bill share a life-long passion, which in addition to their professional lives, absorbs much of their free time. Their separate working lives have recently merged since the opening of the David Attenborough building in Cambridge and they now find themselves commuting to the same work place. Their two daughters have been at school in Cambridge and are as passionate about life and their pursuits as their parents. Anna is a lovely, adventurous and independent young woman. She is a fine singer and has taken many of the solo parts at school. She is now in her second year at Exeter University, reading psychology. Tessa, like her parents, is passionate about animals and wildlife and keeps a menagerie in her bedroom. She is a gifted artist and has already decided that this may be the career she will pursue when she leaves school.

Helena works as a clinical psychologist in Norwich and also, Kings Lynn. She lives with her two children, Joe and Rosy, in the village of Reepham, Norfolk, close to her ex-husband, Rex, (Warner) with whom the children, when they were younger, spent time after school as well as every Saturday night. She manages splendidly as a single mum and sole breadwinner and has provided a lovely, supportive and creative home life for her family. It hasn't been easy and there are times when the burden of a very demanding job and having the main emotional and financial responsibility for her children, has weighed heavily on her. But she has remarkable courage and an adventurous spirit and manages to take a family holiday every summer that the children will always remember. Last year she chartered a yacht in Greece, where they explored some of the Greek Islands. This summer she took the children to Friesland, to sail their Wayfarer dinghy along the lovely waterways of Holland. Joe and Rosy are both fine and have always accepted their double home life and enjoy the added benefits of two birthdays and two Christmases, every year! Rosy is tall, slender, blonde, extremely bright and is a beautiful dancer. Joseph, now over 6', is a high-flyer academically and is a fine, very disciplined young man. He is ambitious and has already set his sights high in terms of a job in the City. He plays the guitar and earns money at the weekends by working as a waiter.

Catherine is married to Roman (Wittig) and they live with their two children, Fynn and Gemma, in Leipzig. They work together as Evolutionary Anthropologists at the Max

Plank Institute, where they both completed their PhDs. Roman now manages the study site of acclimatized chimpanzees, where their students do all their research, in the Ivory Coast. This means that he must spend two (separate) months each year overseeing their students and assistants in the Tai Forest. Roman and Cathy have spent many years together in Africa. In addition to the Ivory Coast, they spent time in the Okavango Delta in Botswana, when Fynn was just two years old. There they lived in a camp that is 50 miles from the nearest human habitation. After Gemma was born they lived near Masindi in Uganda, for two years. When the children started school, it was no longer possible for them to continue living in Africa, so after coming home they worked for a time in St Andrews and from there returned to Leipzig and the familiar setting and social group from their PhD days. The children are both bilingual and happily settled at their International School and in their beautiful home beside a lake. Fynn is 15, 6' tall and still growing and is a fine-looking and athletic young man with a warm and generous personality. Gemma is exceptionally bright, both intellectually and in her glowing presence. She has a compact and supple body and is a fine gymnast. She is loved where ever she goes and from an early age has won everyone's hearts with her sunny personality and winning smile. Unfortunately, Cathy and Roman's jobs are not permanent, so they will soon have to look for jobs elsewhere.

The Baynes Family have not figured so far in this memoir and our relationship with Michael, Jonathan, Carolyn and Andy, the four children of my brother John and his wife Ann, has always been close. When our children were young we saw a lot of one another and exchanged our children during the school holidays and they became an important part of our lives. The cousins were often a welcome relief and visits to each other's homes provided a very different perspective on their lives. For the Crockford girls, it was a revelation to be a part of a mostly masculine environment, whereas for Carolyn, a home full of sisters was often a welcome relief from so many brothers!

They have all grown up to be remarkable people, each outstandingly successful in their different pursuits. Michael is a warm and generous man with a strong Christian faith, which he lives in every aspect of his life and this is shared by his lovely wife, Synthia and their daughter, Tatiana. We see little of them now as they live in Bordeaux where Michael works in the wine industry. Jonny and his gifted Russian wife, Julia, run a successful consultancy business together, in London, which requires a lot of travel and plenty of juggling as their two adorable children, Gabriel and Marianne, are only 5 and 3 years old. Then come the twins, Carolyn and Andy, who have remained close in spite of living very different lives. For many years Andy was working for Google in California, where he lived together with his adorable French wife, Stephanie and his two lovely daughters, Chloe and Isabella. Carolyn has two outstandingly musical sons, Louis and George. Carolyn is an inspirational music teacher in a primary school and has won great accolade with an outstanding Ofsted report. Each of Johnny and Ann's children have, in their different ways, been a splendid and vital part of all our lives.

Photo by Hank Jansen

Diana Baynes Jansen has lived a long and varied life. She has a big family with three daughters by her first husband, David Crockford, and four stepsons from her second marriage to Christopher Jansen. There are fifteen grandchildren from their combined families. She has been widowed twice and now lives alone in the home in Northumberland where she has spent the last 50 years of her life.

Diana works as a Jungian orientated psychotherapist and sandplay therapist. She is the author of an acclaimed biography of her father, H.G.Baynes, (*Jung's Apprentice*), who was a close friend and colleague of C.G.Jung.

She began her working life as a nurse and later studied at the Guildhall School of Music to become a professional singer. After her marriage to Christopher she went to London to train as a psychotherapist. She is still working part time and also has time to write and to enjoy her garden.

Lightning Source UK Ltd.
Milton Keynes UK
UKHW012010250220
359314UK00002B/71